THE ESSENCE OF
TESHUVAH

THE ESSENCE OF *TESHUVAH*

A Path to Repentance

RABBI CHAIM NUSSBAUM

JASON ARONSON INC.
Northvale, New Jersey
London

This book was set in 11 point Bem by Lind Graphics of Upper Saddle River, New Jersey, and printed by Haddon Craftsmen in Scranton, Pennsylvania.

Library of Congress Cataloging-in-Publication Data

Nussbaum, Chaim.
    The essence of teshuvah : a path to repentance / by Chaim Nussbaum.
      p. cm.
    Includes bibliographical references and index.
    ISBN 1-56821-025-6
    1. Repentance—Judaism.   2. Tishri.   3. Repentance—Biblical teaching.   4. Bible. O.T.—Criticism, interpretation, etc.
5. Forgiveness—Religious aspects—Judaism.   6. Judaism—Doctrines.
I. Title.
BM645.R45N87   1993
296.3'2—dc20   93-1226

Manufactured in the United States of America. Jason Aronson Inc. offers books and cassettes. For information and catalog write to Jason Aronson Inc., 230 Livingston Street, Northvale, New Jersey 07647.

Contents

Part III
The Month of *Teshuvah—Tishrei*

ACKNOWLEDGMENTS

Two years ago, my book *Semblance and Reality* was published. I then was busy putting the finishing touches on *The Essence of Teshuvah* and three more books (which should reach the publisher in the near future). I would therefore not have managed to offer *The Essence of Teshuvah* at this moment if not for the encouragement and help of dear friends.

I wish to thank first my editors, Esther Posner and Yaakov Avraham Finkel (himself a successful author), who devoted their efforts to editing *The Essence of Teshuvah* successfully.

Furthermore, I wish to thank my enthusiastic publisher, Mr. Arthur Kurzweil, and his devoted, capable staff, for their efficiency and patience. The members of our publication committee, Dr. Morton Posner and Meyer Weinstock, also took an interest in *The Essence of Teshuvah*.

Most of all, I wish to express my gratefulness to our Creator for a devoted companion in my eventful life, "Dear Rachel," known to the readers of *Chaplain on the River Kwai* (1988), who, after fifty-six years of our marriage, has not ceased to actively, indefatigably assist her life's mate.

INTRODUCTION

Repentance and Forgiveness

One of the fundamental principles of Judaism is the concept of repentance. Its unique theme addresses saints and sinners alike, holding out the promise of complete reconciliation with God. The sages of the Talmud (*Yoma* 86a) poignantly articulate the paramount importance of *teshuvah* when they say, "Great is repentance, for it reaches up to the divine Throne of Glory."

Numerous books have been written on the fascinating subject of repentance and forgiveness, most of them focusing on an analysis of the ways and techniques of achieving repentance and the halachic aspects of *teshuvah*. While the authors of these books admirably deal with the aim they set for themselves—explaining the "how to" aspect of *teshuvah*—there remains a need for books offering a proper understanding of the intriguing phenomenon of *teshuvah*: the essence of repentance, man's sin awareness, the limits of his self-knowledge, and the concept of divine forgiveness, to name just a few. It is questions concerning these topics that occupy the mind of the thinking and searching Jew of today.

This book speaks to the men and women of our generation in an attempt to answer the problems a sensitive student of religion may be pondering.

He or she may be puzzled by such questions as: Why do I regret? Why do I have to verbalize my confessions? How can I, a limited creature living in a finite world, hope to obtain forgiveness from an infinite, remote God Who resides beyond the confines of time and space?

This book attempts to provide answers to these questions. It is divided into three parts that discuss the basic concepts of repentance and forgiveness. Part I deals with the biblical personalities who traditionally exemplify the redeeming power of *teshuvah*: Adam and Eve, Cain, and King David. It shows how these great figures from the distant past struggled with the vices of ambition, greed, and lust. The Bible builds the stories of their triumphs and failings around carefully chosen events in their lives, presented in a few succinct words so that one may discover the common features of their *teshuvah* as well as the characteristics of their specific types of individual repentance.[1]

While Part I analyzes the struggles, successes, and failures of the personalities, Part II concentrates on contemporary man, probing inward into his soul. Among the questions addressed are the reality of conscience and man's awareness of sin. Models are presented to help the reader gain an understanding of such perplexing problems as the following: How can a sinner visualize the fact that the heavenly record of his thoughts and deeds does not become hopelessly scrambled with the accounts of billions of his fellow human beings?

Part III has divine forgiveness as its main theme. Forgiveness is the common thread that runs through all the fall festivals of the month of *Tishrei*: Rosh Hashanah, Yom Kippur, Sukkot and the Closing Days of Shemini Atzeret and Simchat Torah. Many readers may be surprised to learn that while the first two festivals, the Days of Awe, concentrate on contrition over conduct in the year just ended, Sukkot and the

Closing Days represent that aspect of *teshuvah* that is concerned with the resolve to change one's way of life in the
coming year.

Although this book touches on some profound and abstract
themes, the author has strived to make it a practical and
intelligible guide for the general reader, as well as an instructive text for the advanced student of Jewish thought. While
there still may be a few scattered segments that the average
reader may find too technical, care has been taken that such
sections can easily be skipped without interrupting the flow of
thought.

It is the author's sincere hope that those who are able to
devote the necessary time and effort to this fascinating subject
will feel encouraged to help develop the kabbalistic and scientific methods of presentation of the basic concerns of *contemporary* man.

I
TESHUVAH—
REPENTANCE

1
ADAM'S REPENTANCE

REB ZISHA'S LAMENT

The first chapters of Genesis relating the story of the creation of man, his defiance of God's will by eating of the forbidden fruit, and his expulsion from the Garden of Eden provide an inexhaustible source for gaining an understanding of the mysteries surrounding God, man, and the world, as well as the natures of good and evil, reward and punishment, and divine justice. Gnawing questions on these subjects have been probed into throughout the ages by aggadists, kabbalists, philosophers, scholars of the *Mussar* movement and the chasidic masters. They have delved into the secrets contained in the early chapters of the Bible, and their research affords us a glimpse into the realm of the spiritual state of Adam before his act of disobedience and the cosmic cataclysm that followed his first transgression.

What drove Adam, who was God's handiwork and who dwelled in the blissful purity of the Garden of Eden, to disobey God? How could he do such a nefarious deed?

The story is told how the renowned chasidic leader Reb Zisha of Hanipol (1718–1800) once threw his hands up in despair, crying out to the Creator, "*Ribbono shel Olam*, Master of the Universe, I cannot understand or ever forgive myself for having permitted Adam to sin against You. After all, was not my soul part of Adam's soul, albeit a very minor part? Still, You, my Creator, know how every cell in my body fears You and trembles in awe of You. How could I have stood idly by without preventing Adam from committing his fateful transgression against You?" (This story is told by Rabbi Eliyahu Kitov.)

Reb Zisha's anguished cry gives voice to the age-old question of how Adam, with his frail and finite nature, would dare violate omnipotent God's unfathomable will, and how he could accomplish his act of disobedience.

The phenomenon of man's freedom to disobey God, which so deeply moved Reb Zisha, is discussed in philosophical terms by the illustrious kabbalist Rabbi Moshe Cordovero (1522–1570) in his seminal work on ethics, *Tomer Devorah* (Venice, 1589). He wrote that one of the divine attributes revealed to Moses is God's quality of *Nosei Avon*, "Forgiving Sin." Literally translated the phrase means, "He carries sin," as if God Himself *bears* responsibility for the sin. The implication is that God provides man with the energy, as well as the physical and mental resources, to commit the sin. Thus, God becomes, in a sense, an accessory to man's transgression once man has chosen to defy Him.

Viewed in this light, Reb Zisha's agonizing outcry takes on added meaning. How can any person use God's gift of intellect and energy to violate his benefactor's will? In Reb Zisha's view, the act of disobedience of God drastically diminishes the stature of man and evokes in him a sense of deep shame and remorse.

However, upon closer examination, an alternate perspective on the Torah account of Adam's disobedience emerges.

Man's stature, rather than being diminished, may well be elevated by his potential to disobey his Creator. The fact that the first divine interdiction of the "forbidden fruit" presumes the possibility of disobedience suggests trespass to be a natural alternative to obedience.

Specifically, the prohibition against eating from the Tree of Knowledge of Good and Evil was accompanied by the warning that man must accept responsibility for his disobedience. "For on the day you eat from it, you will definitely die" (Genesis 2:17). The fact that God issues a threat suggests that He anticipates the possibility of man's disobedience. You post a warning sign to deter people from doing something you anticipate they might do. The severity of the threatened punishment—death—suggests that God indeed envisioned the possibility of man defying Him.

Should we conclude from the preceding that Adam and Eve were justified in exercising their privilege to disobey God's commandment? If so, how could Eve have decided to risk death, the ultimate form of self-destruction? If she had died on the very day she ate the forbidden fruit, she would not have been able to benefit from her newly gained freedom to choose between good and evil. Her freedom would have proven to be a fleeting mirage.

THE TWO TREES

The answer can be found—as developed later in the text—in the fact that Eve was aware of the regenerative and revitalizing powers inherent in the Tree of Life. Standing in the middle of the Garden on the same site as the Tree of Knowledge (Genesis 2:9), the Tree of Life had the power to repair any consequence of human error or misjudgment. The two trees, which complemented each other, possibly shared a common root: The Tree of Life was the source of *regeneration* of life forces; the Tree

of Knowledge promoted the physical, aesthetical, and intellectual aspects of man's life. Hence, we may conclude that Eve
defied God's command in spite of the death penalty because
she was aware, not only of the existence of the Tree of Life, but
also of the meaning of its God-given name. She recognized that
the name, Tree of Life, implied the power to mend any in-
fringement of one's survival powers and the potential to overcome the aging process. She knew, therefore, that she could
find a remedy for her disobedience and that death was not
inevitable.

THE FEAR OF MAKING ERRORS

The second question we are faced with is this: While it is true
that wrongdoing is not punished by instant death, should
people not be afraid that in making independent and free
choices they are prone to err and misjudge? And we ask
ourselves: Why did this fear of making the wrong decision not
prevent Adam from disobeying God?

Of all creatures in the world, man alone is endowed with a
soul originating in the heavenly realm. Essentially, the soul is
a spark of God. It is the source of man's deep affinity to God
and his inherent desire to fulfill His will. After eating from the
Tree of Knowledge, Adam also received the quality of intelligence enabling him to discriminate between good and evil
independently. Armed with this capability, Adam felt that he
was justified in assuming he could keep to a minimum the risk
of making serious errors, so that he would not jeopardize his
own and mankind's existence and future development by
using his God-given freedom of decision making.

THE NAKEDNESS OF MAN

Adam and Eve disobeyed God in the expectation that they
would become like God, as the serpent suggested: "On the

day you eat from it your eyes will be opened and you will be like Elo-him, knowing good and evil" (Genesis 3:5). It is natural, therefore, that they would compare themselves to the world's non-God-like creatures. However, in their intense desire to appear God-like, they became aware of the nakedness they shared with all animals.

One may wonder, why did they suddenly object to being naked? After all, the Torah tells us that before eating from the Tree of Knowledge they had accepted their nakedness as proper and fitting: "The man and his wife were both naked, yet they felt no shame" (Genesis 2:25). What brought about their change of perception?

Adam and Eve wanted to be God-like; therefore, they expected to look different. By eating the forbidden fruit, "their eyes were opened," their appearance gained in importance, and their initial acquiescence to animal-like nakedness, they realized, had been a mistake. They understood that biologically they were an integral part of the animal world, not only in appearance but also in bodily functions. They recognized that even in their most God-like function—the act of procreation—they seemingly performed like animals. The sublime God-likeness they anticipated to attain by eating of the forbidden fruit did not materialize. They had overestimated their ability to rise above their animal-like nature.

A GARMENT OF FIG LEAVES

In their attempt at becoming like God they made use of their newly acquired God-like creative intellect to *improve* on God's blueprint for Creation: "They sewed together fig leaves and made for themselves loincloths" (Genesis 3:7). The Torah makes no mention of their consulting God regarding the momentous change they wanted to bring about by sewing loincloths. And a fundamental change it was, since it made

man the only creature in the world to wear clothes. Adam and
Eve made the decision to fashion loincloths *on their own*. This
astonishing fact speaks for itself and is indicative of their
implied criticism of God for creating them naked like the
animals.

But in their *enthusiastic* attempt at correcting God's creation,
they overlooked the fact that the garment of fig leaves did not
really satisfy their needs. Fig leaves, belonging to the plant
world, are not a natural part of a human being. Consequently,
the loincloths Adam and Eve fashioned for themselves did not
really change the character of the human body's enclosure;
they were still left with a feeling of nakedness.

It is true that the garment of fig leaves helped to hide the
human body from sight, but it did not fulfill the function of
being a natural enveloping outer skin that actually enclosed
the human body, and the reproductive organs in particular, so
that the human body would at least *appear* different from the
rest of the creatures.

"They went into hiding from God's presence among the
trees of the Garden" (Genesis 3:8). Why did they hide? Were
they ashamed of their nakedness? But they were, at that moment, dressed in their fig leaf loincloths. Yet, the Torah tells
us they were *afraid* (Genesis 3:10) rather than *ashamed*. Indeed,
they were afraid, for it dawned on them that they had misunderstood the nature and scope of the freedom to make decisions. Their failure in their first attempt to improve upon
God's creation convinced them that one does not attain God-
likeness by violating His will, no matter how meritorious
one's intentions are.

Adam and Eve discovered that the loincloths they had
made from fig leaves were unnatural and unsuitable to cover
a *human's* nakedness properly. Within their fig leaf garments they still felt naked. Ironically, it was Divinity Himself
Whom they had attempted to correct, Who with compassion
solved their dilemma for them. In verse 21, "God made leather

garments for Adam and his wife and He made them feel dressed." God thereby pointed out to them that man is biologically unalterably linked to the animal world, and although they had mistakenly attempted to correct an assumed error in His creation, the Creator provides the means of minimizing the embarrassment incurred by man's shortsightedness and lack of understanding.

BLENDING THE GOOD WITH THE GOOD

Creation implies pluralism, separability of created elements. Consequently, both *tziruf* (combining) and *iruv* (mixing) are basic concepts in the story of Creation.

One is accustomed to speaking of *iruv tov vera*, the mixing of good and evil, at the very beginning of the creation of the universe. However, by reading the story of Creation more carefully, we find, at the earliest stage of Creation, not so much a mixing but rather a *tziruf*, a combination of "good and good." Indeed, we are told that in creating man "in His image" (Genesis 1:27), God formed him "out of the dust of the ground, and breathed into his nostrils a breath of life" (Genesis 2:7).

In the process of creating man, God brought about a fusion of the best of all possible substances. In so doing, He initiated the first mixture of heterogeneous elements, combining fertile dust, the most suitable substance for molding man's intricate body, and the *nishmat chaim*, the soul, originating in the heavenly realm. The final product, man, was an amalgamation of *tov vetov*, a lasting bond of good and good, dust of such splendid quality that it became the raw material for building the exquisitely complex human body combined with the divine breath of life. This combination of good and good was ideally balanced and designed to last forever, even without the help of the Tree of Life. (It should be noted that even after

Adam's longevity was drastically cut, he still lived to nearly one thousand years.)

Adam's disobedience disturbed the equilibrium that existed between the dust of the earth and the celestial "breath of life." By acquiring God-like knowledge Adam decided to tip the scale overwhelmingly in favor of the divine soul vis-à-vis the physical body, bringing about an imbalance in God's Creation that would prove to be the underlying cause of death. After man partook of the Tree of Knowledge, his soul's function was magnified to such an extent that it could not be contained any more within the frame of an *estranged* body indefinitely. As the Torah states, "Now he must be prevented from putting forth his hand and also taking from the Tree of Life and eating it and [consequently] living forever" (Genesis 3:22). Thus death, the punishment for eating of the forbidden fruit, was not an arbitrary decree. It was the natural consequence resulting from the disturbed balance in the combination of dust and the divine breath of life. Man, in his attempt to become like God, upset the equilibrium of the *tziruf*, the perfect blend of his earthly and spiritual components. The newly formed imperfect mixture could not last indefinitely. The possibility of man's immortality no longer existed. He was doomed to die. Henceforth, death would be a reality that would always be in the back of man's mind.

In its purest sense, death means reducing the mixture of dust and spirit to its elements. When the reason for death is explained to Adam, the Creator tells him, "You are dust, and to dust you shall return" (Genesis 3:19). In death, the two components, body and soul, having become heterogeneous again, are returned to their original sources: the dust to the earth and the soul to its heavenly realm.[1]

MIXTURE OF GOOD AND EVIL

Adam's misjudgment and the resulting imbalance between the material and spiritual realms brought about a tragic transformation that turned the initial blessed combination (*tziruf*) of good and good into *iruv*, a heterogeneous mixture of good and evil. This blend of good and evil is all-pervasive, extending into all facets of creation. First and foremost, the earth was cursed: "Cursed is the ground because of you; you will derive food from it with anguish. . . . It will bring forth thorns and thistles for you" (Genesis 3:18–19). Thorns and thistles intermingled with wheat barring direct access to its desired produce. Second, nutritional foods contain harmful—even poisonous—ingredients that are especially detrimental in the process of aging. It would become Adam's task to separate and untangle the all-pervasive *iruv*.

ADAM REGRETS

How did Adam react to his failure to "become like God"? He did not deny his guilt, and accepted God's verdict. Interestingly, the Torah's story does not explicitly mention the term *sin* or *punishment* in this regard.

Adam was confronted with the new reality of a cursed earth that his disobedience had brought into being. The mixture of good and evil became evident in the human condition, which is a blend of joy and suffering, of thorns and thistles amid the earth's good fruit, of birth alternating with death. In order to restore the world to the pristine state of Eden, Adam had to undo the consequences of his misjudgment. He had to continue to separate the improperly mixed elements. Man was given the task of promoting the Creation by farming the land, which essentially is a labor of separation: clearing the land of thorns and thistles and setting aside an area for planting crops, segregating wholesome grain and produce from harmful weeds in order to provide nourishment for man. Thus, by cultivating the land and creating order in the midst of chaos, Adam was making amends for bringing about imbalance and upheaval by disobeying God's command.

THE PRESERVATION OF MANKIND

Undaunted by his failure to become God-like and the ensuing realization that he would not live forever, Adam presented a confident vision of the future: "The man named his wife Eve (*Chavah* in Hebrew, from the word *chai*, meaning life) because she was the *mother of all life*" (Genesis 3:20).

Adam thereby ensured that the divine gift of life would go on. Although God decreed that Adam and Eve were destined to die, mankind as a whole would not perish. Eve became the symbol of the indestructibility of life. As the mother of all life, she was the builder of the future of humanity, which must continue the primordial process of separating good from evil, step by painful step.

THE FUTURE GENERATIONS

The first new link in the continuation of mankind was forged with the birth of Seth: "Adam lived 130 years, and he had a son in his likeness and image (*bidmuto ketzalmo*)" (Genesis 5:3).

The wording of this verse bears a striking similarity to "God said, 'Let us make man in our image and likeness (*betzalmeinu kidmuteinu*)'" (Genesis 1:26). The obvious symmetry points to a basic parallel between God's creation of man and Adam's role in perpetuating mankind. While God's initial plan was for Adam to live forever, according to the apparent intent of the Torah's story, Adam's misjudgment brought death into the world. Still, Adam made God's plan of immortality a reality by securing—through the process of procreation—the perpetuation of life and the survival of the human species.

The Torah thus underscores both Adam's and Eve's roles as the progenitors of mankind, she "the *mother* of all life" (Genesis 3:20) and he the *father* of all mankind, begetting offspring "in his likeness and image" (Genesis 5:3). This unusual emphasis may suggest that Adam and Eve saw the beginning of a promise of success in their attempt to repair the damage they had caused by their tragic error in judgment. The Torah's story implies that Adam and Eve brought forth new generations to complete their task of *berur*, of separating good from evil.

ADAM'S *TESHUVAH*

The Torah's account of Adam's disobedience makes no mention of Adam's *teshuvah*, repentance, or of divine forgiveness for his act of disobedience. In fact, according to the *Midrash*, on two occasions God asked Adam to repent, to which he replied, "*Ee efshee*" ("I won't do it"). Unlike Cain, Adam was not willing to accept a new mission on earth and change the direction and meaning of his life. But just as *teshuvah* means return, Adam *did* return to his Creator, attempting to fulfill his God-given assignment; thus he did "do *teshuvah*."

His way of "doing *teshuvah*" was and would remain unique. It could be described as threefold in character:

First, he accepted unquestioningly his punishment of "By the sweat of your brow you will eat bread" (Genesis 3:19). Originally, after placing him in the Garden of Eden, God assigned Adam the task "*le'ovdah uleshomrah*" ("to work the earth and to guard it") (Genesis 2:15). When the earth was cursed after his transgression, however, Adam's task was made immeasurably more difficult. Nevertheless, for the nine centuries of his life he discharged his task conscientiously and with admirable diligence.

Second, consistent with his loyalty, Adam started making amends for his disobedience and began repairing the rift between God and man.

Third, realizing that he could not in his lifetime complete the task of restoring Eden and releasing the totality of sparks of

goodness from the clutches of evil, Adam resolved to perpetuate life by bringing into being new generations. He hoped
that mankind eventually would purge itself of his transgression and bring about the ultimate redemption.

But how would this be accomplished?

Before his act of disobedience, Adam, the most perfect of
God's creations, lived in close communication with his Creator, Who guided him every step of the way, prodding and
admonishing him, asking, "Ayekkah?" ("Where are you?")
(Genesis 3:9). After his transgression, however, his relationship with his Creator changed, since God, as it were, withdrew from him. Henceforth, Adam could no longer depend on
the Creator's *constant counsel*. Instead of guiding him, God
would leave him to his own devices. He would let him rule the
world through *trial and error*. Ruling the world, however,
entailed separating good from evil. Thus man would be left to
grope in the dark in his search for good or, as the kabbalists put
it, in his desire *lehidamot lekono*, to be God-like, attempting to
extricate the sparks of sanctity that are imprisoned in the realm
of man's self-assertion. But did he believe he could succeed?

Adam did try to explain his disobedience by telling his
Creator, "The woman that You put at my side—she gave me
of the tree, and I ate" (Genesis 3:12), implying that Eve was
given to him to be a fitting and trustworthy helpmate.

Where did he go wrong? Should he have refused the food
she offered him? Although Adam offered an explanation for
his disobedience, he did not argue over the punishment meted
out to him.

Eve followed the same pattern, asserting that she never
would have dreamt of initiating any disobedience toward her
Creator. It was the serpent that made her do it, she claimed, by
appealing to her judgment. Where did she go wrong? Was it
wrong for her to use her understandable ambition to be God-
like in making her decision? Again, there is no mention of any
argument over the horror of the punishment she received. By

tempting Eve, the serpent had started it all. Therefore, unlike Adam and Eve, the serpent was *not* asked why it had committed its misdeed.

The Torah's account makes it clear that disobeying God is not justifiable, not even on the grounds that someone else was the cause. Defiance of God is punishable despite the fact that one received contrary orders or advice. Still, in such a case there is at least room for mitigation (which is proven by divine forgiveness).

This is a basic rule in the history of man: being served the forbidden fruit or being told to do the forbidden is at best a mitigating factor. It is essential, with freedom of decision, to resist temptation, to act according to the divine commandment in any conflicting situation.

In the future, it will be possible for man to bring a sacrifice and receive forgiveness for a sin committed inadvertently, where man can offer a valid excuse.

ARE MAN'S EFFORTS DOOMED TO FAILURE?

Now we are faced with a puzzling question. Can man, who is free to determine what is good and bad for him and for the world, ever hope to arrive at a program of overcoming the basic causes of sin: personal pride, greed, and lust for power? Can he ever hope to find the purity of goodness and disentangle it from the morass of evil in which it is mired? Is he not doomed to failure from the very start? With a guesswork approach of trying and failing, of ups and downs, can man ever hope to attain the ultimate goal of final redemption?

Theoretically, yes, he can indeed. While it is true that most trials end in failure, the experience man gains from his failures makes him wiser and increases his success rate in future attempts. The remarkable advances in science and technology

offer clear evidence of the efficacy of research through the
method of trial and error.

Thus, Adam could indeed have believed that man is justified
in hoping to reach the goal of redemption through his own
efforts. He apparently did not ask for divine assistance.

DIVINE REVELATION

Summing up, the Creator, concerned with the well-being and
success of His Creation, must have realized, of course, that
man, at crucial junctures in history, would be in need of divine
intervention, or otherwise be destroyed. Whenever man
would err, God would reveal Himself to him in order to guide
him on the path toward redemption. Already at the very
beginning, in the case of Adam, He intervened by revealing to
him his error of covering himself with fig leaves and clothed
him instead with animal skin.

When ten generations came and went, and Adam's attempt
at mending the world did not accomplish its goal, culminating
in the Flood, the Creator made a covenant with Noah and
revealed to him the seven Noachide Laws as guiding lights for
mankind's conduct.

Ten more generations faded into oblivion, and once again
God revealed Himself to Abraham, selecting him to become
the father of a nation that was to bring to completion Adam's
mission of restoring the ideal state of Eden by serving as a
model to humankind's nations.

The climax of divine revelation was reached when God on
Mount Sinai chose the nation of the descendants of Abraham
as the recipient of His Torah, in its written and oral forms. The
Torah is the guidepost that shows the Jewish people and
universal humanity the way toward the messianic age, when
the cosmic balance that was upset by Adam's misjudgment

will be restored. Through the Torah, Adam's *teshuvah* of continued mending will come to fruition, when the blinding glare of *iruv* (confusion) will be dimmed and *berur* (clarification) will be accomplished. Then "God will be King over all the world; on that day God will be one and His name will be one" (Zechariah 14:9).

2
CAIN'S REPENTANCE

Few chapters in the Torah can match the drama and attendant perplexity of the story of Cain and Abel. As the tragic account unfolds, we are overwhelmed by baffling questions. What prompted the heinous crime of fratricide at the dawn of history? Why did God accept Abel's offering and reject Cain's? What was the basic flaw in Cain's thinking? A careful study of the Torah's text will yield illuminating insights and shed new light on these and other problems.

When the earth was cursed in the aftermath of Adam and Eve's misstep, Cain and Abel were confronted with the harsh reality of having to work in order to sustain themselves. To be sure, the trees were still overfilled with an abundance of fruit that provided certain types of food for a long time. Nevertheless, looking toward the future, Cain, the practical realist, vigorously plunged into the task of working the cursed earth, producing food to ensure the survival of mankind. He saw himself as the divinely appointed *"oved adamah"* a "tiller of the soil" (Genesis 4:2).

Abel viewed the world from a different perspective. He

considered it his task to preserve and nurture life on earth, to be a *ro'eh tzon*, "feeder of flocks" (Genesis 4:2), a shepherd. A visionary idealist, he dreamt of being the guardian of God's world and took upon himself the unproductive job of raising and caring for God's creatures, the animals. (Eating meat was forbidden at that time and was sanctioned only after the Flood [Genesis 9:3]. Thus, tending flocks served no nutritional purpose.)

Essentially, the tasks Cain and Abel assumed were a reflection of their respective weltanschauung: Cain labored for the benefit of man, while Abel toiled for the sake of God's Creation.

Cain ungrudgingly went about his backbreaking work of wresting nourishing vegetation from a resistive earth covered with thorns and thistles. Totally committed to improving the physical condition of man, whom he considered master of the earth, Cain was God's quintessential egocentric creature.

By contrast, Abel engaged himself in the gratifying occupation of tending the gentle flocks, a vocation that leaves the shepherd ample time for contemplation of God and nature, and for introspection, enabling him to elevate his soul to the nearness of the Creator. (It is no coincidence that the Patriarchs, Moses, David, and many of the biblical prophets were shepherds.) Abel perceived his mission as attempting to unite the physical and spiritual worlds into an uninterrupted continuum. He was the epitome of an idealist.

"At the end of days" (Genesis 4:3), having gathered in his first harvest, Cain recognized that the Creator had allowed the cursed earth to provide sustenance for man. Gratefully, he offered God a sampling "from the fruit of the soil."

"Abel also brought an offering to God: some of the first-born of his flock and from their fats. God paid heed to Abel and his offering, but to Cain and his offering He paid no heed (Genesis 4:4–5)."

The inescapable question immediately arises. Why did God

accept Abel's offering while rejecting Cain's? For an answer let us take a closer look at the gifts the two brothers offered.

A significant difference becomes apparent in the nature and quality of the two offerings and in the attitude thereby manifested by the giver. Cain's offering consisted of a *random* sampling of the food that the earth—cursed though it was— produced for man who toiled at cultivating it and segregating the grain from the weeds. With his offering, Cain recognized God as the Creator Who nourishes the world and grants it life. As he thanked God for allowing man to partake of the finest he can extract from the earth, Cain felt it to be inappropriate to offer the choicest produce when it was God's intention for *man* to enjoy the best. Indeed, the man-centered Cain set aside the best for man. Abel the idealist, on the other hand, offered God of his best and fattest sheep, the product of his painstaking effort and tender care, as a demonstration of his devotion to God's creatures.

GOD'S REJECTION OF CAIN'S OFFERING

When God rejected Cain's offering, Cain was shaken to the core. Overcome with anger and gloom, he considered himself a victim of a miscarriage of justice. After all, had he not worked his fingers to the bone, defying thorns and thistles, to make the world livable for man? He argued that Abel's work of tending sheep, although done with tender care, was of no benefit to man. In his view, the ultimate aim of God's design for the world was the physical well-being of man, as the Psalmist would later proclaim, "The heavens belong to God, *but the earth He gave over to man*" (Psalm 115:16). And Abel had done nothing to promote man's welfare and prosperity.

Before Adam's transgression, Cain may have agreed with Abel's vision of a God-centered world. But after the Creator withdrew His *berachah*, His boundless blessing, and gave over the world to man, Cain did not consider his brother's lofty dream of a God-centered world to be a tenable and viable option any longer. How could man ever hope to overcome the curse of the suffocating overgrowth of thorns and thistles—the manifestation of the universal *iruv*, the mingling of good and evil—if he did not view the world as man's exclusive domain and commit himself completely to mankind's survival through material advancement?

By accepting Abel's offering, God indicated that, even after Adam's act of disobedience, man's destiny was to be God-centered, while Cain's man-centered view must be given no more than secondary consideration.

Cain became furious and deeply depressed. Over the period that he had been struggling with the earth to obtain his first fruits, he had no inkling that his nutritional, man-centered view was wrong and that Abel's idealist approach was the correct one. He now received a rude awakening and felt the resentment of a man whose life's work had crumbled to dust.

It was true that God had rejected Cain's man-centered philosophy, but with deep compassion He showed him the way to put things right—the path of redeeming repentance. Turning to Cain, God asked, "Why are you angry? Why are you depressed? Surely, if you do right there is uplift; but if you do not do right, sin crouches at the door" (Genesis 4:6–7).

Cain was given a clear-cut choice. If he would disavow his man-centered outlook on the world, he would be restored to his previous position as Adam's firstborn son, and his chosen profession of tilling the soil would enjoy equal status with that of Abel's keeping flocks and herds. On the other hand, should he persist in his erroneous view, "sin crouches at the door," or to put it in simple terms, jealousy and ambition would inevitably lead him to commit criminal acts.

Cain had to make a decision. Would he retain his man-centered view of the world or would he bow to God's demand that the world be God-centered? He reasoned that certainly no compromise was possible between the two ideologies. Man-centeredness and idealism could not exist side by side. It had to be one or the other.

Following the example set by his parents, who violated God's command by eating from the forbidden tree, Cain disregarded God's directive. Casting aside God's admonition to be uplifted by doing good and accepting God's choice, he chose what *he* deemed to be to man's advantage: perfecting the world for man's benefit and comfort.

Comparing his opposition to God's will with his parents' transgression in Eden, Cain realized, no doubt, that his situation differed markedly from theirs. Adam and Eve, constituting all of humanity, had decided jointly and unanimously on what was good for man, in blatant contravention of God's will. Their transgression meant that all mankind was rebelling against the Creator.

While his parents shared the same outlook, Cain's philosophy was opposed by his brother. Moreover, Abel's view had the explicit backing of God. Cain, in opposing his Creator, found himself in the unenviable position of being a dissenter. To avoid defeat in an unequal struggle he had to eliminate the opposition. He had to destroy his brother.

WHERE IS YOUR BROTHER ABEL?

After the murder, God asked Cain, "Where is your brother Abel?" "I do not know," Cain replied. "Am I my brother's keeper?" (Genesis 4:9).

The denial sounds childish and dishonest. Cain obviously knew Abel's whereabouts. It is unthinkable that he would not be interested in his *only brother and fellow being's fate*. There must be a cogent reason for Cain's bland response to an omniscient God.

His denial of responsibility for his brother manifests the

arrogance of the self-righteous. Cain's "I don't know" must have implied that the Creator should not have asked him this question. Voicing his earth-centered doctrine, he reproached his Creator. "Don't you realize I'm busy," he seems to say, "fulfilling my task of tilling the soil, all by myself, with no one to lend me a hand? Unlike Abel, I cannot show concern for anyone. Caring for others would detract from my total commitment to promoting the physical well-being of mankind, Your creatures. Do You not see that I cannot be expected to be *anyone's* keeper, not even my brother's?"

CAIN'S FATAL ERRORS

Cain's disastrous fratricide stemmed from a serious flaw in his outlook on life. This flaw blinded him to the truth and was the root of his errors.

Primarily, he harbored the misconception that the world was either God-centered or man-centered and that the two ideas were mutually exclusive. The truth is that there is a place for both positions. In fact, they are intimately linked to each other: after the severing of their original unity, the spiritual clearly takes precedence over the material.

Cain compounded his error by failing to understand that since his ideology had been rejected by God, he could not build a harmonious relationship with the Creator by pursuing his man-centered program in defiance of God's will.

One error led to another. In the wake of his crime God told Cain, "The voice of your brother's blood is screaming to Me from the ground" (Genesis 4:10). Cain failed to understand that his "brother's blood" was symbolic of Abel's unfinished task, which cried out to be fulfilled and completed.

Tragically, Cain did not comprehend that the violent end of Abel's task would also terminate his own assignment. He did not understand that his chosen vocation of tilling the soil was an adjunct to Abel's primary task of elevating the world. He did not grasp that any lasting success he could achieve would be due to Abel's work of bringing all of Creation closer to the Creator.

Cain did not realize that he was the beneficiary of the overflow of the abundant heavenly blessings that streamed to Abel. His successful harvest had led him to believe that his man-centered approach was favored by God and that the elimination of Abel's view might therefore be welcomed by the Creator.

With Abel's death, the God-centered world view had lost its champion. However, since Cain's man-centered ideology derived its vitality from Abel's idealistic view, it collapsed in the absence of its life-giving source. Cain's efforts at cultivating the soil, detached from the Creator's special care, failed as the earth ceased to nurture his crops. He was told, "When you work the ground, it will no longer give you of its strength" (Genesis 4:12).

Mistakenly, Cain thought that by removing his brother he put an end to Abel's ideology. Abel's idealistic vision, however, did not evaporate. It endured in the Creator's memory and was brought back to life in Adam's third son, Seth, who was born to Eve "in place of Abel, whom Cain had killed" (Genesis 4:25).

ALIENATION

Cain was thus alienated from the earth and barred from doing the work that gave meaning to his life. He was no longer able to combat the encroaching jungle of thorns and thistles or harvest food from an increasingly hostile and unyielding earth. Though Cain had lamented his loneliness before, with Abel removed from the scene he was overwhelmed by a sense of utter desolation. He was stripped of his purpose in life, banished from his native soil, and condemned to be "a restless wanderer" (Genesis 4:12).

REGRET

Convinced at last that his reasoning was faulty, and filled with newly gained insight born from experience, Cain uttered a moving cry of despair, a plea that has a familiar ring to the contemporary reader. He exclaimed, *"Gadol avoni minneso"* ("My sin is too great to bear") (Genesis 4: 13). I have sinned against my brother, against myself, against the earth, and against God. I have destroyed my brother's life and in so doing I have ruined the roots of my own life. What I have done is intolerable to the Creator and to the earth that now rebels against me for I am the destroyer of the life of a human being created in the image of God.

It is significant to note that in this plaintive lament Cain characterized his misdeed as *avon*, a purposeful sin. By contrast, the Torah does not define Adam and Eve's transgression as *avon*. In conventional rabbinic terminology, Adam's sin is characterized as the *cheit* of *Adam Harishon*. A *cheit* is an inadvertent sin, a missing of the mark, an error in judgment. Cain committed an *avon*, an intentional crime of destroying a human life.

Rashi (1040–1105), taking an aggadic approach, detects a nuance of protest underlying Cain's words of despair and regret. He rewords Cain's outcry as "Is my sin then too great to be forgiven?" Cain implied that his sin, as grave as it was, should not be beyond forgiveness by the Creator. If God would prove to be capable of condoning the crimes of mankind and the rivers of blood shed in the wars of human history, why could He make no concession for his one regrettable crime? Why could He not pardon his single act of murder, which was motivated not by personal hatred but by a desire to promote the well-being of humanity?

Cain became a restless and rootless wanderer on the earth. In anguish he poured out his heart to his Creator, giving vent to his despair: "Behold, you have banished me from the face of the earth" (Genesis 4:14) so that there is no place for me to fulfill my assignment, which was my sole channel of communication with You, my Creator.

Cain apparently realized that in the future many people would kill their fellowmen. Consequently, God would have to countenance innumerable murders. Could his Creator not overlook his single act of murder?

Cain expressed with perceptive clarity the source of the pain of his tormented soul when he lamented, "I will be hidden from Your presence" (Genesis 4: 14).[1]

Cain felt that he had attained closeness to the Creator by fulfilling his God-given task of tilling the earth. Having been banished from the earth and barred from his assignment, he was out of touch with God, cut off from His kindness and deprived of the warmth of the divine light.

His misfortune sprang from another error in the long string of Cain's misguided notions. In disobeying God he had counted on some measure of divine displeasure and retribution, but never imagined that he would be condemned to suffer *total* estrangement from his Creator.

TESHUVAH

Uprooted and alienated from the Creator, Cain faced up to the seriousness of his crime and decided to embark upon the process of repentance. He accepted the tragic life of *na venad*, restless wandering, cut off from the source of his spiritual sustenance. Since he had destroyed a life possessed of the divine spark, however, he was convinced that he had forfeited the right to his own life as well. Fearfully, he turned to God, asking Him for protection against blood avengers seeking to kill him. "Anyone who meets me may kill me" (Genesis 4:14), he cried.

Surprisingly, the Creator agreed to protect him against any *go'el hadam*, blood avenger, by placing a mark on him, which would make him unassailable by man or beast.[2] God even went beyond offering protection, issuing a warning to any potential slayer: "Indeed, anyone who kills Cain will be punished seven times as much" (Genesis 4:15). It is as though Cain had been declared innocent of unjustified premeditated murder.

A NEW MISSION

Cain settled in the land of Nod, a name denoting nomadic instability. He reached a compromise with God. As the sages put it, Cain told his father, *"Nitpasharti"* ("I have come to terms, I made a deal with my Creator"—*Bereishit Rabbah* 22). Accepting his alienation from the earth, he agreed to make no attempt at disobeying God by surreptitiously cultivating the land. Instead, he took on a new task. In Nod, the land of instability, he found his new mission in life: he became a *boneh ir*, the builder of a city (Genesis 4:17).

Working by himself without the benefit of tools—they were not yet invented—Cain set out to build a small hamlet, arduously erecting house after house, building workshops, until gradually a settlement emerged, the nucleus of a city. He built the city for his son, who was permitted to farm the land and who needed shelter and protection from the elements for himself and his family. Cain, however, being a builder, remained detached from the soil. His new career brought an end to his wanderings, although his inner restlessness was not alleviated.

Interestingly, Cain's personality had undergone a marked change. Building a city and providing shelter implies caring for one's fellow man. Cain, the city builder, was no longer the same man who callously asked God, "Am I my brother's keeper?" He had become his fellow man's guardian and expressed his new attitude by naming the city not after himself, as might have been expected, but "after his son Enoch" (Genesis 4:17).

Thus Cain's *teshuvah* meant not only profound regret but first and foremost a drastic reversal in his character, reflected by a shift in his attitude toward his fellow man, a fact that proved to be of crucial importance to all future generations.[3]

Indeed, Cain's new, somewhat altruistic way of life may have served as an example for his descendant Lemech, who had three sons and one daughter. One son was the first man to fashion copper and iron implements, tools that greatly eased the drudgery of the farmer. The second built tents for cattle herders. The third invented the harp and the flute, which help relieve the stress and gladden the spirit of the hardworking man. And according to the *Midrash*, his only daughter, Naamah, was an exceptionally beautiful woman.

Thus, Cain's descendants, each in his own way, enhanced man's enjoyment of all the elements contained in the Tree of Knowledge (*maachal*, production of *food*; *taavah*, possessive *enjoyment* of the arts; and *nechmad, beauty,* beauty being a basic value in God's universe). This may be an indication that the severity of the curse of the earth would ultimately be mitigated.

In summation, we have seen that initially Cain refused to repent fully, emulating his father before him, who defiantly would have continued to eat from the Tree had he been permitted to continue living in Eden. Cain was unwilling to abandon his vision regarding man's relationship to his Creator. After committing fratricide he realized the enormity of his crime and that he would have to die as the inescapable retribution for his *avon* of murder. To avoid death he made a deal with the Creator. He repented and accepted the painful punishment of being barred from tilling the soil, which was tantamount to renouncing his life's basic ideology.

By *unselfishly* building a city for his descendants, who were not barred from working the earth, Cain proved the sincerity of his repentance. More importantly, by safeguarding the interests of his fellow men—although they were all members of his own family—he dedicated himself to a task that was acceptable to the Creator, and thereby established a new channel of communication between himself and his Creator.[4] True, his new mission was no longer one of *innovating*, *creating*, and *producing* ("*le'ovdah*"), but it did have the characteristics of *preserving* and *protecting* the old and tried ("*leshomrah*") (Genesis 2:15), and safeguarding the world for his fellow men against whom he had so grievously sinned.

While Cain expressed his *teshuvah* by redirecting his life, thereby removing the barrier that had separated him from his Creator, he was and remained the prototype of the rebel against God, the epitome of the anarchist who throughout history has risen up against established law and order and divided human society. He set the example for the hedonism and *chamas* (violence) that prevailed in the era before the Flood in a society of men whose members were not necessarily closely related. By refusing to accept the death penalty for killing his brother he may have set a precedent for the insensitivity toward mass murder and genocide that has pervaded society from its earliest beginnings until the present time.

In closing, we must not overlook a redeeming feature in the biblical story, hinting at the possibility of viewing Cain as a partner in man's seemingly endless path toward *tikkun*, the final restoration.

An aggadic commentary offers a surprising sequel to the story of Cain and Abel. According to this source, Na'amah, daughter of Lemech, a descendant of Cain, married Noah, the survivor of the Flood. Lemech, as was mentioned earlier, was a descendant of Seth, whom Eve considered a worthy replacement of Abel. Thus, in a remarkable display of ultimate divine forgiveness, the offspring of Cain and Abel were united jointly to implement God's master plan to ultimately "mend" the world, which still deeply suffers from the mix-up of good intentions and the reality of bad choices.[5]

3
DAVID'S DILEMMA

WHO IS DAVID?

We now skip approximately twenty-five centuries to discuss King David. Aggadic sources consider David the man who was destined to finally complete the process of mending and restoration—*tikkun*—that was begun by Adam when he was driven from Eden.

The personality of King David presents a strange dichotomy. On the one hand, he is the divinely elected messianic king, a man whose soul bespeaks the ultimate in moral refinement. The "sweet singer of Israel" (2 Samuel 23:1), he is the author of history's most widely read literary creation, *Tehillim*, the Book of Psalms. On the other hand, reading the biblical account, we encounter David the military commander and brilliant strategist who subdued his enemies with iron-fisted determination and secured a lasting peace for the Land of Israel.

Who was the real David and what were the sources of his apparently contradictory character traits? For a better understanding of David's human qualities and motives, let us explore in depth the biblical record of his life.

THE JEWISH MONARCH

The role of a Jewish monarch is governed by the royal charter outlined in Deuteronomy (17:14–20). The Torah views the king as a humble person whose conduct inspires the people to greater attachment to the Torah and the observance of *mitzvot*. He is the messianic ruler who ushers in an era of justice and morality.

After the age of the Judges came to a close and the people asked for a king who would have the privileges of a contemporary king, the prophet Samuel proclaimed a contemporary royal charter "for a king to govern Israel like all other nations" (1 Samuel 8:5). This granted the monarch absolute authoritarian power (1 Samuel 8:11–17).

David, aspiring to live up to the ideals of the Torah's mandate, had the fervent desire to build a House for God. He envisioned the erection of the *Bet Hamikdash*, the symbol of God's presence on earth, as the culmination of his reign.[1] It was to be the crowning achievement of his glorious career and was the driving force at the core of his being.

But it was not to be. The prophet, speaking in the name of God, announced to him, "You have shed much blood and fought great battles; you shall not build a House for My name, for you have shed much blood on the earth in My sight" (1 Chronicles 22:8).

The prophet made it clear that David was not disqualified from fulfilling his aspiration because of any personal sin he had committed, but as a direct consequence of the numerous wars he had fought. These bloody conflicts were the source of much inner conflict and bitter anguish that overshadowed David's life.

DAVID'S DUAL CHALLENGE

Ascending the throne, David was fully aware that the Torah stipulated that the Temple could be built only when peace and justice prevailed in the country and its borders were safe and secure from invading enemies. Hence, he was confronted with a dual challenge: First, in order to establish peace in the land he had to defeat the enemies situated inside as well as outside its borders.[2] Second, as the messianic king he had to find a way to combat the enemy in accordance with the principles of justice and fairness mandated by the Torah's royal charter.[3]

To be sure, being a king in his times, David had the privilege to exercise the totalitarian rights conferred upon him by the royal charter of Samuel.[4] Indeed, like his predecessor, Saul, he began his reign by governing with a modest posture, in the spirit of the Torah charter. But unlike Saul, whose attitude later changed, David attempted until the end of his life to abide by the principles of humility, fairness, justice, and compassion, principles he extended to embrace even his enemies. Unfortunately, times were not ripe for David's messianic form of warfare. It should come as no surprise, therefore, that his idealism was perceived by his military commanders as unrealistic, if not downright irrational.

David had to convince his officers and men of the validity of his messianic view. To accomplish this while fighting a war was a formidable task. To achieve victory on the battlefield, a fighting man must outdo his enemy in cunning and ruthlessness. Would David's combat-hardened warriors be inclined to adopt his idealism and a lenient attitude toward their adversaries? How could they possibly understand David's benevolent attitude toward Saul, who was determined to eliminate him? How could they appreciate the fact that David did not kill Saul when he had opportunities to do so (1 Samuel 24:6–7)?

How were tough fighters to understand David's moral

tactfulness and delicate sensitivity when he poured on the altar the water that was brought to him by his officers at great personal risk? Although terribly thirsty, David refused to quench his thirst with water for which his men had jeopardized their lives (2 Samuel 23:15–17).

On the other hand, David must have appeared insanely harsh to the messengers who brought him the "good" tiding that they had killed his rival to the throne, Ish-Boshet, son of Saul. Instead of being rewarded for their initiative, they received the death penalty for killing a righteous man anointed by God (2 Samuel 4:5–12).

DAVID'S TUMULTUOUS LIFE

David encountered his greatest difficulty when dealing with the vicious intrigues within his own royal court that may have arisen in response to his high-minded approach to the affairs of state.

An example of the turmoil that beset David can be found in the story of the killing of the eighty-five priests of Nob and their families. Briefly, this is what happened.

Fleeing from King Saul, who relentlessly pursued him, David received provisions from Achimelech, the priest in the city of Nob. He was also given the sword of Goliath. Do'eg, the head herdsman,[5] who happened to be in Nob on a spiritual retreat, witnessed how David was aided by the priests, and he reported to Saul that the priests had given supplies to his archenemy, David. Saul thereupon ordered Do'eg to retaliate by killing all the priests of Nob along with their families (1 Samuel 21: 2–10, 22:9–23).

In a way, David felt responsible for the deaths of the priests. He blamed himself for accepting the food and the sword of Goliath in the presence of Do'eg and for failing to foresee the trouble his actions would engender. And when Evyatar, the sole survivor of the massacre, arrived at David's camp, David felt morally obligated to let the young priest know that he had been aware of Do'eg's presence, stating, "I am to blame for all the deaths in your father's house" (1 Samuel 22:22). He thereby exposed himself to his adversaries, who pounced on him, faulting him for his idealistic policies. Worse than that, he placed himself at the mercy of the young escapee priest who would one day change loyalties.[6]

Opposition to David surfaced again when Jo'ab, his commander in chief, treacherously killed Abner, Saul's general (2 Samuel 3:27). David was suspected by his enemies of plotting the elimination of this commander who had fought for a rival king.

Jo'ab killed another general, Amasah, the former commander of the army of David's rebellious son Absalom (2 Samuel 20:10), whom David had chosen to replace Jo'ab. In fact, David found himself surrounded by an inner circle of military men and politicians who in their hearts cast aspersions on the sincerity of his motives and attributed his actions to nefarious schemes. In particular, the politicians, his main adversaries, cast doubt on the sincerity of the king's magnanimity.

TORN BY INNER CONFLICT

David's virtue came under a cloud once again when his critics suspected him of having had a hand in the death of a number of Saul's descendants. These descendants were murdered by the Gibeonites, the Temple servants who claimed that they had been persecuted by Saul, having been falsely accused of siding with the priests of Nob (2 Samuel 21:2-6).

One opponent, Shimi ben Gera, a member of Saul's family, went so far as to hurl stones at David, cursing him: "Get out, get out, you *man of blood*, you villain! God is paying you back for all your crimes against the family of Saul, whose throne you seized. God is handing over the throne to your son Absalom; you are in trouble because you are a man of blood!" (2 Samuel 16:5–8).

This was an extreme statement, suggesting that the young messianic dreamer had turned into a bloodthirsty king and was now rejected by his Creator. Shimi's curse may have sounded convincing since everyone remembered that God had taken away the monarchy from Saul because God did not approve of his conduct as king. Shimi implied that David's monarchy would be transferred to Absalom, for David's bloody reign displeased God.

Shimi purposely shouted his accusations in the presence of David's few remaining friends, who were ready to defend their king against Absalom. Yet David, the champion of truth and justice, ignored the fact that Shimi was trying to undermine their loyalty to him. He countered their protestations by apologizing for Shimi: "Let him go on hurling abuse, for God has told him to" (2 Samuel 16:11). He did not permit his courtiers to kill Shimi and later, when David returned to the throne, strange as it may seem, he forgave Shimi for his sedition and blasphemy.

To recapitulate, we have thus far attempted to illustrate David's idealistic conduct as a king, true to the Torah's charter of Deuteronomy (17:14–20).[7] However, just as Saul had been before him, David was later compelled to deviate from the Torah's charter and adopt some of the authoritarian privileges granted the king by Samuel's charter.

Thus we find David more deeply involved than ever in his military campaigns. We discover that in his dual role as messianic king and head of the armed forces, David was too weak. He was unable to convince his political and military appointees that his messianic approach, based on his faith in God, was effective in winning wars. He could have pointed to his personal victories as proof that his idealistic perspective was the only realistic course to follow. Indeed, history would buttress his argument for conducting wars along the lines of the To- rah's mandate. He could have cited his successes against his enemies, beginning with his miraculous victory over Goliath, continuing through the victories in all his great battles, up to the successful military campaigns of the great trans-Jordanian wars. He could have demonstrated how, against all odds, he had subdued his enemies because his warriors were the sol- diers of God who enjoyed divine providential protection.

As the scope of his military campaigns against Ammon, Mo'ab, Aram, and other enemies broadened, however, he could not maintain personal control over his field com- manders and exhort them to fight in keeping with the ground rules of Torah ethics and morality. Without direct contact with the troops, his personal charisma dwindled. His influence was further weakened when, despite repeated attempts, he failed to replace such independent military leaders as Jo'ab. As a result, he was held responsible for Jo'ab's ruthless tactics in waging war.

DAVID'S PROBLEMS

Aggadic sources point to another of David's apparent failings: by fighting longer wars, he triggered moral laxity among the troops. It is suggested that he was held responsible for the hundreds of brutish fighters in his personal entourage, who were assumed to be his children by "captive women."[8] The sages comment that both Absalom and Adoniyahu—David's sons who sought to overthrow him—were born of captive women.[9]

Remarkably, despite the devastating effects of protracted warfare, David's personal messianic vision did not die. David, and later Solomon, emphasized that in time of peace the blood of innocent people must not be shed under any circumstances.

This points to a highly developed sensitivity to bloodshed and murder in the everyday life of a people that had become accustomed to the death toll of the battlefield. David personally set the high moral tone by proclaiming that the shedding of innocent blood was an indelible stain on his throne.

Moreover, in a society based on Torah laws, any grave injustice would be considered a capital crime. When Nathan the prophet told David that a rich man had taken his poor neighbor's only sheep and prepared it for his guest, "David flew in a rage against the man and said to Nathan, 'The man who did this deserves to die' " (2 Samuel 12:5).

One may argue that banning bloodshed in peacetime while tolerating it in time of war is a license to indiscriminate killing on the battlefield. Indeed, this was the case in Jo'ab's great military campaigns. But due to David's moral authority, the tragic reality of bloodshed on the war front did not universally affect the moral climate at home. Surely this was a remarkable accomplishment.

Nevertheless, on balance, David, the inspired man of God, was overshadowed by his role as the warrior king.[10]

David realized at last that he was no longer in full control of his men. It finally dawned on him that the army that had started out as the "army of the living God" (1 Samuel 17:45) had suffered from *iruv*, the confusion and commingling of good and evil, of semblance and reality. The undaunted fighter who had never known fatigue suddenly became tired in the heat of battle—"*vayaaf David*" ("David grew weary") (2 Samuel 21:15).

The Bible relates that David was overcome by physical fatigue as he was leading his men in a battle against the Philistines. A Philistine suddenly lunged at him and would have killed him, had his field commander not come to his aid.

His physical tiredness may have also been triggered by the fact that Jo'ab, his general, had disobeyed him. Jo'ab had loyally served David and defeated the armies of David's rebellious son, Absalom. Yet he defied David's strict order to spare Absalom's life, killing him in cold blood.

Deeply shocked by David's close call, his officers vowed that the king, their inspiration on the battlefield, would not go out into combat any more, lest "the lamp of Israel" be extinguished. Significantly, David did not object.

DAVID'S DISAPPOINTMENT

What the reader of David's story may not realize is that the prophetic narrator, in typically biblical fashion, is hinting at a fundamental change in the king's life. In passing, he is telling us that David concentrated on his messianic mission in the latter part of his life. Henceforth, he would no longer project the image of a warrior. He had assumed this military posture when he fought Goliath, relying only on God, to the extent that he spurned Saul's offer of protective armor. He wanted to instill in his men this messianic spirit of fighting a war. He realized, however, that he could not imbue his army with this attitude of total dependence on God. While his general staff was comprised of capable men who were loyal to their king, they obeyed him only as long as his orders did not interfere with their own pragmatic views of waging war.[11]

David's failure to indoctrinate his generals with an outlook on waging war based on the Torah's principles of justice and morality led to the heartbreaking tragedies that later plagued his life. It fostered the bloodshed that kept him from fulfilling his life's greatest ambition: the building of the *Bet Hamikdash*.

DAVID THE *BAAL TESHUVAH*

Up to this point we have attempted to present a portrait of a king whose messianic vision of justice and universal peace

clashed with the brutal realities of warfare. We will now show
another facet of the king's spiritual makeup: David the *baal
teshuvah*, the returnee to God.

In the wake of the intensity of the *iruv* and the commingling
of good and evil in his environment, David succumbed to the
pressures of the prevailing militaristic ideology. His fervent
idealism gradually cooled off, which led to misjudgments in
his conduct of war and eventually to weariness and complete
physical exhaustion.

As could be expected, after a lifetime of uninterrupted
warfare, the callousness of combat infected David's personal
life. When he heard the prophet's verdict, "That man is you!"
(2 Samuel 12:7), he fully realized that he was the wealthy man
in the parable who slaughtered the only lamb his poor
neighbor Uriah the Hittite possessed (David took Uriah's
wife, although he already had eighteen wives). He was the
man who had finally decided on the solution to eliminate
Bathsheba's husband, Uriah.

I HAVE SINNED

Still, David responded to the prophet's admonition with a
straightforward admission of guilt: "*Chatati*" ("I have sinned
against the Lord") (2 Samuel 12:13).

The reader must be impressed with the forthrightness of
David's confession, where he could have invoked royal im-
munity or self-defense as an excuse. We stand in awe of
David's self-knowledge. What agonizing inner struggle must
have raged in the heart of a man as sensitive as David as he
probed the depths of his prodigious mind to uncover his sin
and the way to repentance.

Thousands of years have passed since this event, yet David's
psalm of repentance (Psalm 51) still echoes the inner struggle
that tormented his soul. Although its moving words show the

world a *new* path away from sin toward repentance and forgiveness, they have the ring of the plaintive lament of an
anguished, broken heart.

At the outset we note that his confession is addressed only
to God. He cries out, "Against You alone I have sinned"
(Psalm 51:6). It was God Who had designated him as the king
who would fight *milchamot Hashem*, the wars of God. This
proved to be an impossible task. Although David was the
consummate idealist, firmly dedicated to establishing a
kingdom of justice and peace, he was overwhelmed by the
fires of *iruv*, of confusion and hypocrisy. The decades of
warfare needed to pave the way, for the building of the
Temple had blunted his sensitivity to his God-given mission
to do battle in keeping with messianic criteria.

The prophet's condemnation of "You are that man!"
shockingly made him aware of his growing remoteness from
God. He saw the truth and suddenly realized that, driven by
the dark forces of *iruv*, he had strayed from his Torah-ordained
charge of being a king of justice and consistent kindness. But at
no time did he renounce or abandon his task. Therefore, unlike
Adam and Cain, whose assignments on earth were changed
after their transgressions, David's task of building the Creator's universal sanctuary, which constituted the essence of his
life, *never* changed.

But having violated God's trust, it was *he* who needed
change, and he prayed, "Fashion a pure heart for me, O God,
create in me a steadfast spirit" (Psalm 51:12). Deeply contrite,
he asked God to grant him the spiritual fortitude to resist the
constant temptations and pressures to which he was exposed
in the pursuit of his messianic vision.

TOTAL REPENTANCE

David's repentance may be defined as *total* repentance. Not
only did he decide to change his conduct, but he was the first

sinner who actually prayed to God for the gift of a changed heart and a renewed personality. The charismatic young hero, the beloved of God, seemed to have turned into a vulnerable, vacillating, guilt-ridden man.

The prophet pronounced the terrifying punishment that would be meted out to David: "Therefore, the sword shall never depart from your house. . . . I will make a calamity rise against you from within your own house . . . even the child about to be born to you shall die" (2 Samuel 12:10–14).

David was oblivious to these appalling curses. They made no impact on him; it was as though they had not been uttered. Since his repentance was not motivated by fear of punishment but sprang from genuine love of God, it was the purest form of *teshuvah me'ahavah*, repentance out of love.

This being so, David did not ask for mitigation of his punishment, as Cain had done, but rather for a complete cleansing of his tainted soul. He prayed, not that the crimson red of his offense be merely bleached to a lighter shade and made less conspicuous but, "Wash me till I am *whiter* than snow" (Psalm 51:9).

What David was asking no other sinner before him had ever requested: to attain a level of innocence greater than his level of innocence before the sin. This plea for transcending whiteness (innocence) mirrored the special quality of his *teshuvah me'ahavah*.

So strong was his new resolve that he was not frightened by the horrifying punishment that was in store for him. His only concern was reaching a level of repentance at which sinning would be virtually unthinkable.[12]

While it is true that David did not succeed in definitively limiting the expansion of wars and wiping out every vestige of corruption and violence, he did prepare his son to be the harbinger of the message of peace, justice, and wisdom.

In his final address, he distilled his philosophy of the mission of a Jewish king into one poignant phrase: "*Moshel baadam tzaddik, moshel yir'at Elohim,*" "He who rules men must be just, ruling in the fear of God" (2 Kings 23:3). A Jewish king must be a righteous man, not swayed by emotions and selfishness, but guided by the fear of God's justice.

This credo he triumphantly flaunted in the faces of those who for many years had scorned his messianic vision of leadership, in the firm belief that his son Solomon would make these principles a reality.

This message, everlastingly inscribed in the Bible, represents David's victory over the arrogant forces of political and military pragmatism of his era.

4
AFTER REPENTANCE

Once he has repented, how should the former sinner deal with the memory of the transgressions of the past? Should he banish them from his mind and look confidently toward the future, or should he continually grieve over his past wrong-doings?

In Psalm 51, the great psalm of *teshuvah*, David makes a significant statement in this regard. He says, *"Chatati negdi tamid"* ("I am ever conscious of my sin") (Psalm 51:5). This seems to indicate that David chose the path of inner torment and self-affliction as his method for preventing the recurrence of sin. Indeed, the biblical account seems to bear this out. When the child to whom Bathsheba, Uriah's wife, had given birth became critically ill because of David's sin, David prayed and fasted for seven days, lying on the ground (2 Samuel 12:16).

In light of this, we might expect David to have reacted in a similar fashion to his sin of causing the death of Uriah, namely, by repenting through self-inflicted suffering. We would pre-sume that, stricken with remorse, he would not have even

considered marrying Bathsheba, but rather would have completely removed her from his life. To our surprise, we are told
that he *did* marry her, evidently choosing an alternative path of
repentance.

Moreover, David's later years were not marked by mourn-
ing, contriteness, and self-mortification to the extent that
might have been expected from a person who claimed he
would never forget his sin.[1]

The truth is that David's postrepentant life combined the
two extremes: the harsh path of self-punishing contrition,
which is evident in many of his psalms, and the positive
outlook of a sinner who has been cleansed and reborn. The
synthesis of these opposing approaches is quite unique. How
strongly David sensed that his way of repentance was indeed
novel and promising is evident from his stated wish to serve as
a model for others. "*Alamdah poshe'im derachecha*" ("I will teach
transgressors *Your* ways, that sinners may return to *You*")
(Psalm 51:15). This verse attests to David's confidence and
optimism. He was convinced that his way of repentance
would appeal to sinners and induce them to return to God.

Predicated on David's declaration that he would never
forget his sin, one assumes that he had chosen the way of
asceticism and self-flagellation to prevent stumbling into sin
again. While David himself did not choose this path, it is the
well-known way of repentance recommended in traditional
sources. It was the custom in certain kabbalistic schools, as
well as within the fifteenth-century chasidic movement in
Germany, to prescribe for a penitent a period of exile from his
home and a number of fast days tailored to the type of sin he
had committed.

It appears, however, that the primary course followed by
David in the case of Bathsheba was to view himself in a
positive light, as a sinner who had been forgiven and whose sin
had been blotted out. This outlook was advocated by some
leaders of the central European chasidic and *Mussar* move-

ments of the past two centuries, who stressed that by continually reliving his past sins, the repentant might, in fact, vicariously enjoy the sweet taste of the forbidden fruit all over again. For example, if one savagely beats a person he dislikes and in repenting re-creates the episode in his mind, in every gory detail, he might be giving vent to his suppressed anger and arouse again his innate viciousness. Thus, despite the appearance of regretful repentance, he is actually rekindling and relishing a dormant sadistic inclination rather than uprooting it.

Indeed, a number of leaders of both *Chasidut* and *Mussar*, the two great movements of spiritual revival, and Rabbi Samson Raphael Hirsch, who led a revival in western Europe, frowned on the practices of prolonged fasting, asceticism, and self-mortification.

An interesting anecdote is told involving the Chafetz Chaim (Rabbi Yisrael Meir Hakohen Kagan, 1839–1933), the universally recognized saint and towering Torah scholar. Once he was approached by a student of his *yeshivah* who had lost his self-control with a young woman. The brokenhearted student asked his illustrious master how many days, spread out over a number of years, he ought to fast in order to attain divine forgiveness for his transgression. The Chafetz Chaim suggested that were he to fast for many days his studies would suffer; instead he recommended that the student choose a sublimated form of fasting by observing a "fast of the tongue." During this "fast of the tongue," in order to avoid spreading *lashon hara* (gossip and slander), he was not to utter even one unessential word. By concentrating on abstaining from talebearing while avidly studying Torah, his soul would be thoroughly cleansed and he would shut out the memories of his sin. This idealized form of fasting is preferable by far to dwelling on the sins of the past.

After his intense repentance, by readily accepting all harsh punishments, David exemplified the ideal *baal teshuvah* who has a positive perspective and enjoys his status without brooding about past transgressions. Still, we are faced with the paradox inherent in his statement, *"Chatati negdi tamid,"* that he was constantly aware of his sin.

An analogy will help reconcile the apparent inconsistency. Imagine a sinner who desecrated the Sabbath for many years. He eventually repents and restores the Sabbath in his home to its full glory. Each Sabbath when he sits down at the beautifully set, gleaming white Sabbath table, looks at the radiant Sabbath lights, recites the *Kiddush,* and sings the Sabbath songs, he realizes *how infinitely happier he* is now than he has ever been before. Instead of agonizing over the desecrations of the past and imposing harsh punishment on himself each Sabbath, he ecstatically enjoys the blessed atmosphere of the holy day each week. True, he will never forget the emptiness he suffered in the past. However, these memories will not evoke infinite sadness; they will enhance his present joy. In this sense, the memory of his sin-filled past serves as a positive stimulus to remain steadfast in his repentance. In no way does it have the negative connotation of self-castigation.

TRANSFORMATION

A new perspective on the problem of how a *baal teshuvah* is to deal with his past emerges: the principle of transforming memories of sin into inducements for happiness. It is this principle that David must have had in mind when he said, "I am ever conscious of my sin." The memory of his forgiven sin made him recognize his present state of divine favor, propelling him to higher levels of spirituality and bliss.

Nevertheless, on reflection, the question still remains unanswered. How does the principle of transformation of sin apply to the case of David and Bathsheba? How can we compare

David's marriage to Bathsheba with the glow of happiness
generated by a regained pure Sabbath?

The answer: Bathsheba was an integral part of David's
messianic mission. The Talmud states that Bathsheba was
destined to be David's wife *misheshet yemei bereishit* (from the
very beginning of Creation) (*Sanhedrin* 107a).

Thus, by being married to her, David was, in fact, fulfilling
God's plan. Seeing Bathsheba was a source of indescribable
happiness to David for he considered their union to be the
actualization of the divine design.

We understand that many critical students of the story of
David may consider this explanation an apologetic act of
whitewashing. Nothing could be further from the truth. A
reading of the *p'shat*, the simple meaning of the text, suggests
that of all David's wives, Bathsheba was chosen to be the
mother of Solomon, the wisest of men, heir to the throne, the
one who would bring to fruition David's messianic task and
continue the Davidic line of succession.

Not Abigail. We would have expected Abigail to be the
mother of David's heir. After all, she was the one who
uniquely stood out for her understanding of David's messianic
role. On their first meeting she defined David's mission in life.
Moreover, she succeeded in restraining him from killing her
husband and shedding blood needlessly. Significantly, David
praised her prudence and blessed her for restraining him from
"seeking redress in blood by my own hands" (1 Samuel
25:18–35). Tragically, in Bathsheba's case bloodshed was not
avoided. In spite of all this, it was Bathsheba who was chosen
to be the mother of the heir to the throne and the progenitor of
the messianic lineage, while there is no mention of Abigail or
her son ever having aspired to the throne of David.

Ironically, Nathan, the prophet who initially severely chas-
tised David for marrying Bathsheba, announced God's
approval of this marriage by adding the name Yedidyah,
"beloved of the Lord," to Solomon's name, demonstrating to

all that this infant (conceived after his mother was widowed) was favored by God (2 Samuel 12:24).

Was God contradicting Himself? Not at all. The prophet made it clear that although David had been wrong in marrying Bathsheba, nevertheless, since she was destined to be an integral part of David's mission, the proper course for David to follow was to repent sincerely but to keep her as his wife. Divorcing her would have meant thwarting God's design. David would be made to suffer gravely for acting impetuously, but he was to remain married to the woman who was preordained to be his wife.

IMPATIENCE

Indeed, impatience and impulsiveness were the root causes of David's sin. The prophet emphasized that David should have waited until the moment arrived that he would be permitted to marry Bathsheba. Indeed, Abigail, when faced with a similar situation, dissuaded David from becoming involved in a forbidden contact with a married woman. As a result of her prudence, David was able to marry her lawfully, as a widow, without shedding the blood of Nabal, her boorish husband, who was committed to Saul and an enemy of David.

David should have reasoned that just as Nabal died of natural causes, Uriah too could die without David's or Jo'ab's direct involvement, or that Uriah might decide at a future point in time to divorce Bathsheba, allowing David to marry her legally. But David knew that Bathsheba was not meant to be Uriah's wife and that she was destined to be married to him.

By being impatient, David *prematurely* brought about the realization of the divinely ordained plan. While his rashness was reprehensible and was condemned by the prophet with the words "You have spurned Me" (2 Samuel 12:10), the end result—his marriage to Bathsheba—bore God's approval.

Clearly, David's sin was impulsiveness,[2] but certainly not adultery, according to certain talmudic opinions. Had he committed adultery with Bathsheba, his subsequent marriage to her would have been prohibited (according to the Oral Law, a man cannot marry a woman with whom he has had an illicit relationship). God would not have approved of it. In fact, David's relationship with Bathsheba was an exceptional case since from the beginning of time she was destined to be not Uriah's but David's wife.[3]

To recapitulate: by David's staying married to Bathsheba, his repentance took on a redeeming quality. He became the role model for a positive form of postrepentance, whereby the sins of the past serve to catapult the *baal teshuvah* to the lofty heights of *deveikut*, attachment to God.[4]

5

THE CONTEMPORARY ROAD TO *TESHUVAH*: NATHAN BIRNBAUM

Teshuvah is not only a thing of the past; it is as valid and effective today as it was millennia ago. Proof of this is the life of Nathan Birnbaum, a latter-day man of *teshuvah*.

Nathan Birnbaum, one of the builders of modern Judaism, in his relentless pursuit of the truth, found himself and his world mired in a morass of materialism, totally estranged from God. He had the fortitude to turn away from fame and prestige. Choosing the God of the Jewish people, he returned to the source, the Torah.

He described his personal odyssey in one of his numerous publications, "*Von Freigeist zum Gläubigen*," "From Freethinker to Believer" [1920]) and wrote a major work, "*Gottesvolk*" ("The Nation of God" [1917]), in which he bared his soul. It is an inspired work addressed to the people chosen by their God. The book made a profound impact on many freethinking Jews who had been taken in by the spurious doctrine of materialism. Seduced by this philosophy, they had become "pagan Jews," "Jews without Judaism," as Birnbaum characterized them, Jews who did not have the courage to or were unable to discover their God.

Nathan Birnbaum was born in Vienna in 1864, the son of parents who had immigrated from Galicia. He was only nineteen years old when he founded Kadimah (Forward), the first Jewish nationalist students' association, in 1883, a full decade before Herzl emerged on the Jewish scene. Dissatisfied with the moral and material rewards of his legal practice, he dedicated his life to improving the status and outlook of the Jewish people. To that end he published *"Selbstemanzipation"* ("Self-emancipation" [1885]), a journal in which he set forth his ideas for a national homeland for the Jewish people.

When Theodor Herzl convened the first Zionist Congress in Basel, Switzerland, in 1897, Nathan Birnbaum became the theoretician and secretary-general of the new movement. (In fact, it was Nathan Birnbaum who coined the name *Zionism.*)

Before long, Birnbaum, an outspoken Jewish nationalist with a burning love for the Jewish people, broke with the political Zionism of Herzl. Convinced that the millions of destitute and downtrodden Jews languishing in eastern Europe could not wait for the establishment of a Jewish state in Palestine, he became an advocate of *galut* nationalism, which strove to settle Jews in countries such as Argentina and Canada, instead of concentrating efforts on achieving nationhood in Palestine.

Subsequently, Birnbaum ran for a seat in the Austrian parliament as a delegate from Lemberg, a city with a large Jewish population. Thwarted by the machinations of non-Jewish politicians, he failed in his election bid. During his election campaign, however, he came into close contact with the Jewish electorate in Galicia. For the first time in his life he discovered the essence and the soul of the Jewish people.

Throughout his life Birnbaum was a firm believer in the tenets of socialism and dialectic materialism. He went so far as to adopt a pseudonym, Mathias Acher, after the renegade of the Tannaitic era, suggesting that he espoused the original Acher's heretic ideas.

Birnbaum, the misguided but utterly sincere idealist, found to his surprise that the Jewish people was inspired not by atheism and socialism, but by a deeply rooted religious faith, by a celebration of life based on a fervent belief in God. But his intellectual honesty and a degree of false shame did not permit him to submit to his new discovery and become a man of *teshuvah* overnight. In a slow and agonizing process of return to his historical roots, he began to study Yiddish, the language of the Jewish masses in Poland. In the process he studied Judaism. After an intense, three-year quest for the truth, he became convinced of a reality that he had sensed intuitively all along but had not fully absorbed. It became clear to him that the Jewish people is God's nation and that Jewish history reflects Godliness and cannot be explained in terms of materialistic philosophy.

This realization led him to the inescapable conclusion that he must personally return to the God of the Jewish people. It was certainly not easy for a man forty years of age to start putting on *tefillin* (phylacteries). Birnbaum found a wise and understanding teacher in Rabbi Tuviah Horowitz, a descendant of Rabbi Naftali of Ropshitz (1760–1827), one of the great chasidic masters. With deep sensitivity Rabbi Horowitz introduced him to the daily routine of *tefillin*, helping him to place them on his arm and head and apply the straps in the proper manner.

Thus Birnbaum, a remarkable man of *teshuvah*, did not enter into *teshuvah* repenting grave misdeeds or immoral acts. He was not the penitent who, burdened by an unbearable weight of wrongdoing, longs for the pure life and seeks to carve out a niche for himself among the devout and the unblemished. He was not primarily reaching for personal redemption or seeking to attain personal closeness to God. It was neither fear of death nor a feeling of emptiness that comes with a life without God that motivated him to choose the Jewish way of life. Remarkably, he was fascinated by his discovery of the God of a holy people, this magnificent nation that breathes and lives its God.

His personal return to God was a logical step for a man of his uncorruptible integrity. Years after his first encounter with God, his commitment to truth led him to return to the unique teachings of Jewish tradition. (It is true that he still needed an emotional experience. He was helped in this regard by living through the awesome and majestic force unleashed by a raging storm he witnessed on a sea voyage across the Atlantic. During that tempest he finally had a close encounter with his God, not only rationally, but also emotionally. The experience transformed him into a full-fledged *baal teshuvah*.)

And because of his commitment to the truth, he would not passively and uncritically accept his newly discovered faith. Unlike the modest and unassuming *baal teshuvah* of our days, who usually is prepared to accept devoutly and immediately any demands of his new faith, Birnbaum rigidly tested and judiciously examined the people of his "new faith"—the vast community of Torah-observant Jews he had learned to love so deeply. He still wondered whether their undeniable compassion was sufficiently consistent. Did it extend to all of God's creatures? He pondered whether the lack of external order and beauty in their daily lives of poverty and *galut* was not a reflection of inner disharmony.

He further asked himself whether the masses of secular and assimilated Jews realized that as the "people of God" they were ordained to be "a kingdom of priests and a holy nation" (Exodus 19:16). He reasoned, therefore, that in order to carry out their mission as a holy people they needed to organize as an assembly of men and institutions in the historical mold of *Knesset Yisrael*, a properly constituted and organized Community of Israel.

He formulated his ideological program based on three principles: first, *daat*, a pure knowledge of God, thereby avoiding all contaminants of assimilation to contemporary paganism; second, *rachamim*, emulation of divine mercy by responding to the physical and spiritual pain of all of God's creatures; third, *tiferet*, emulation of divine splendor by striving for beauty, harmony, and purity in the entire sphere of life. He abhorred the distortion and ugliness that had crept into Jewish life as a result of living in exile under the intolerable conditions imposed upon Jews by their host nations. In his fiery soul these three principles took on an aura of *kedushah* (sanctity) so that he spoke of the *kedushah* of *daat*, knowledge and pure faith; the *kedushah* of *rachamim*, compassion; and the *kedushah* of *tiferet*, splendor, orderliness, and beauty, both in society and in each individual's life.

To implement his vision of an organized and functioning *Knesset Yisrael*, Birnbaum demanded a radical change in Jewish life. For centuries the Church had helped its adherents strangle Jewish economic development by excluding Jews from agricultural work and the guilds (associations of artisans). To undo the detrimental results of these restrictions, he called for the establishment of Jewish settlements outside the big cities, so that Jews could earn their livelihood by farming, raising livestock, and working in the trades through a broad-based program of *Berufsumschichtung* (retraining).

Was Birnbaum an unrealistic dreamer? He denied it. He saw enormous potential for the realization of his plan in the mass emigration to North and South America and Canada from eastern Europe. Unfortunately, this emigration was not planned and supervised (except, of course, for the few who chose to live as *chalutzim* [pioneers coming to *Eretz Yisrael* to live and work on a *kibbutz*] in Palestine). Hundreds of thousands found their way into the metropolitan centers of the North American continent, where they absorbed the prevailing culture. Despite their move to a country of freedom and unrestricted opportunity, the structure of their economic life did not change in the New World. They remained storekeepers, peddlers, and *luftmenschen* (unsuccessful traders). Instead of turning to farming, as Birnbaum had envisioned, these immigrants assimilated and many of their children intermarried and lost their Jewish identity.

A similar plan to Birnbaum's was launched by the Jewish Colonization Association (ICA). Founded in 1891 by Baron M. von Hirsch, the organization established agricultural colonies for new immigrants in Argentina, the United States, Canada, and Brazil. The overwhelming majority of immigrants, however, paid no attention to the efforts of the ICA movement and were totally unaffected by it.

It pained Birnbaum, the compassionate observer of his people, to see a historically unique opportunity go to waste. His practical ideas had been rejected by the Jewish masses, who were in the grip of secular socialism. Their failure to seize the hour was a tragedy that pained him for the rest of his life.

He then realized that before Jews would be willing to change professions, they would have to undergo a change in outlook and attitude. Birnbaum, a man who formulated his ideas in prophetic language, now put his efforts into creating an intensely religious movement, which he called *Olim* (Ascenders), and which he hoped would bring about a change in people's weltanschauung within the scope of the three *kedushot* (sanctities). He furthermore berated the religious Jews for their weakened messianic fervor and the resulting threat of sterility and stagnation.

THE *OLIM* MOVEMENT

The aim of the *Olim* movement was the building of *Knesset Yisrael*, which would be the instrument for the realization of the social and political aspirations of a "healthy" Torah-observant nation. This was a program for the spiritual rebirth of God's nation.

His appeal was so novel and so intense that it aroused a strong emotional response in many thinking individuals. Yet, it received a cool reception on the part of the bureaucracy of the major religious political movements. Surprisingly, some chasidic leaders treated Birnbaum's ideas with reserve despite professing interest and even enthusiasm. They sensed that Birnbaum intended to create a new movement, which would not be an offshoot or a natural development of the mighty chasidic movement, which to them represented the soul of the Jewish people. Furthermore, many felt that a *baal teshuvah* ought not criticize contemporary Torah-observant Jews, much less suggest changes in the perceptions of Torah life. The *chasidim* were intensely happy with their lot and were not looking for new attempts at salvation.

More than once, when speaking to me, Nathan Birnbaum quoted Psalm 51:15, "I will teach transgressors Your ways, that sinners may return to You." He explained that while communism, Bundism, Yiddishism, and the effects of assimilation were threatening the survival of chasidic and Orthodox Jewry in general, Torah-observant Jews did possess a great deal of vitality and enthusiasm, which gave them a false sense of security and let them think they were immune to the blandishments of these pernicious influences. Hence, they did not feel the urgency to look for new ideas in order to stave off the progressive weakening of Torah-observant Jewry. Birnbaum remarked, somewhat cynically, that the time was not ripe for his call for renewal. The urgent call for change would only be heeded once Torah-observant Jewry suffered further losses. He realized that only a strong *teshuvah* movement would rejuvenate Torah-observant Jewry.

Disappointed at the anemic response to his call, he did not fully realize that *Chasidut*, rather than growing weaker, was actually flourishing and gaining new adherents. And even in western Europe, where Torah Jewry had indeed shrunk to a small minority, Torah observance was on the upswing, growing in numbers and influence. In eastern Europe, *yeshivot* and Orthodox school systems were producing a young generation intensely dedicated to Torah ideals.

Ironically, much of the growth in power and prestige of Orthodoxy was due to the impressive stature of that great *baal teshuvah* Nathan Birnbaum and his following. Already in those years one could feel the stirrings of change. People, albeit not in large numbers, responded enthusiastically to the *Olim* idea. Although his *Olim* movement did not appeal to the masses, his prophetic voice and call for renewal found a sympathetic ear among the younger generation of leaders. Being fully absorbed in finding an optimum solution for religious and social renewal, he did not sufficiently perceive the change his prophetic language and breadth of vision had brought about. And indeed, despite certain reservations, the Gerer *rebbe*, the most popular leader in the chasidic world, with over one hundred thousand adherents, as well as the heads of great *yeshivot* (Telshe, Slabodka, and others) recognized Birnbaum's historical influence on contemporary religious Jewry.

Numerous committed idealists were willing to take an active part in the movement, leading personalities like Yehudah Leib Orlean, director of the Central Beth Jacob Teachers' College in Cracow, an impressive figure and devout original thinker. Eliezer Gershon Friedensohn, publisher of the influential *Beth Jacob* monthly journal in Poland, was also deeply impressed by Birnbaum. In Lithuania, Rabbi Shmulevitz of the Telshe Yavne Teachers' College and editor of the scholarly monthly *Hane'eman* was an ardent admirer of Birnbaum. In Poland, Leibel Fromm, the theoretician of the Poalei Agudath Israel (the worker's movement of Agudath Israel), was a great admirer of the *Olim* movement. In Germany, it was Jacob Rosenheim, the ideologist and president of Agudath Israel World Organization, who wrote about Birnbaum in glowing terms. Also among Birnbaum's fervent adherents were a number of prominent rabbis, publicists, and essayists, including the *baal teshuvah* poet Eliezer Schindler and the Dutch industrialist C. H. B. van Leeuwen of Rotterdam, also a *baal teshuvah* and a director of the giant Unilever Corporation, who was Birnbaum's main financial backer. In the *yeshivah* of Heide near Antwerp, Jacob Bronner and writer and journalist Moshe Tchechoval founded an *Olim* center that generated a great deal of enthusiasm. In light of these auspicious grassroots beginnings one may assume that, if not for the tragic destruction of the Holocaust, the *Olim* movement might have grown to become a creative force in Jewish life.

Birnbaum, the passionate realist, never tired of writing, publishing book after book and essay after essay, never giving up hope. Through his unflagging efforts he reached an ever-widening circle of individuals, writers, and journalists who were inspired by his words. Writing long before the age of the word processor, he set down his thoughts three lines to a page: at the top, center, and bottom. This allowed him to edit, correct, add, and delete, weighing each word, reshaping each sentence, creating a literary masterpiece.

Birnbaum's repentance was unique in its clarity and rationale. "I did not seek God," he wrote. "I did not have to find Him. He suddenly announced Himself to me and entered into my consciousness." He must have become aware, especially at the end of his life, of the wide gap that existed between the magic of his spreading influence on individuals and the almost complete lack of response on the part of the masses and political organizations to the reality of the *Olim* dream.

The *Olim* movement demanded from people a patient and honest self-appraisal, an evaluation of the sincerity of one's actions and beliefs, and the development of a sense of social orderliness and beauty. These were the prerequisites for creating a change of heart, mind, and values in the potential *oleh* (ascender). Of course, such high standards of moral and ethical behavior would severely limit Birnbaum's appeal to the masses. This may explain the slow pace of Birnbaum's new form of *teshuvah* to attract a massive following.

It is true that our generation is witnessing the amazing movement of repentance. Is this movement choosing Birnbaum's way of emulating Abraham in building altars and calling mankind and Jewry *"beshem Hashem"* ("in God's name"), to worship the Father of the Jewish people and the Creator of the universe (Genesis 12:8)?

Most contemporary returnees to Torah observance come back to God as individuals seeking out God, Who will grant them peace of mind, and Who will give meaning to their lives. They are seeking out God and are in awe of all that Torah-observant people accept as the proper way of life.

Does this imply a basic criticism of the spirit of return that is prevalent in our day? Are the many thousands of *baalei teshuvah* wrong in courageously effecting a more or less sudden change, rebuilding their personal lives based on a deep-seated longing for God and the Torah way of life? Is their *teshuvah* flawed because it is not always steeped in messianic dynamics?[1]

A number of *baalei teshuvah*, including Israeli actors and Soviet émigrés, address people via the media and at international conventions. They tell their stories of *teshuvah* but do not admonish and criticize. They rarely (and even then, not publicly) offer ideas to remedy unhealthy conditions in the Torah-observant world, as Nathan Birnbaum, who never tired of reproving and educating, had.

It is true, however, that the fiery enthusiasm of contemporary *baalei teshuvah* has exerted a surprisingly strong effect on families and friends. They have a weighty share in the growth of the current *teshuvah* dynamics.

The truth is that their *teshuvah*, which springs from a personal yearning for their God, is historically authentic and based on examples of the past. The contemporary men and women of *teshuvah* find themselves in good company. History's greatest penitent, King David, fighter for justice and messianism, is at the same time the prototype of the individual repenting sinner.

As a warrior, elevated to leadership straight from tending his father's flocks, David characterized his army as "the army of the living God" (1 Samuel 17:26, 36). Later in life, he cried out as an individual, "My soul thirsts for You, my body yearns for You" (Psalm 63:2). He also composed the following moving passage:

> One thing I ask of You, O God, only that do I seek: to live in the house of God all the days of my life, to gaze upon the pleasant harmony of God and to frequent His Sanctuary. (Psalm 27:4)

David, who sought Divine bliss, appeared on the arena of history as a fighter against evil. In his later years he set his sights to building the house of God, where he would dwell and experience the personal exultation of the divine presence. (Until the Temple was built God's presence dwelled in the Tabernacle, the tent of the ark.)

Nathan Birnbaum, the great *baal teshuvah* of our time, like David, who was propelled by his thirst to achieve justice and happiness for his people, proclaimed the authority of the God of the Jews, and challenged them to keep before their eyes the messianic vision "to advance with the Law, through the attainment of holiness, to the coming of *Mashiach*." Broadening his message, he even called on all believers in God the world over to join the Jewish people in fighting materialism and atheism.

THE *TESHUVAH* FAMILY

It is obvious that a family with grown children whose head has returned to Torah observance at a mature age is faced with difficult and crucial choices. Such a family was that of Nathan

Birnbaum. The common traits that distinguished the members of the Birnbaum family were their integrity and tenacity. How did they react to the dramatically delayed turnabout in Birnbaum's spiritual life at over forty years of age?

His wife Rosa was a comely lady with an impressive bearing. (I often witnessed how passers-by would turn their heads in admiration when this handsome couple walked the streets of beautiful Scheveningen, the Netherlands.) To fully adapt to the Torah way of life at an age of past forty years must have been far more difficult for her than it was for her sons, who had been teenagers when their father changed. In breaking with her past, she was not just an obliging and obedient wife to her husband. She sincerely and completely accepted the new obligations *Halachah* imposed upon her as well as the relative poverty into which the family was plunged despite her husband's capacity to earn a good livelihood as a professional.

Husband and wife made the journey together. Because of Birnbaum's lifelong closeness to his wife, he shared his ideas with her so that during the years of his inner struggle, she progressed along the same path as he, although at a different pace. When his gradually changing views led to his acceptance of the halachic way of life, she was equally ready for it.

His journal "*Selbstemanzipation*" ("Self-emancipation"), the first German-language publication expressing nationalist ideology, drew the ire of the assimilated Jews. They considered it dangerous because it could be read by non-Jews, who would find out that Jews did not consider themselves Germans but rather fiery Jewish nationalists. As a result, except for the subscribers' fees, he received no remuneration.

His entire family worked hard addressing and mailing the journal. The editorial and administrative offices were housed in the various drawers of his modest furniture. Thus, the family living on a tight budget was even deprived of the privacy of their small home.

NATHAN BIRNBAUM'S THREE SONS

Birnbaum's three sons were Solomon, a paleographer (an expert at deciphering ancient writings); Menachem, a businessman and artist; and Uriel, a painter and poet.

Solomon was close to twenty years old when his father fully accepted the daily duties of an observant Jew. He held his father's image contantly before his eyes. Like his father, Solomon was not interested in amassing money as a practicing architect. He dedicated his life to the study of Yiddish, the language of the Jewish people his father loved so much. Until his ninety-ninth year, Solomon never ceased writing on paleology and Yiddish, even devising a new system of spelling Yiddish (which was adopted by Friedensohn, publisher of the widely read *Beth Jacob* journal, and by several Orthodox publishers of textbooks). He raised his entire family in the halachic traditions.

Menachem, an artistic soul, could not accept his father's belated *teshuvah*. He had an inkling that his father was patiently waiting for the day that he too would sense the feeling of closeness to God, perhaps when Menachem turned forty, the age his father received the call.

Menachem would jokingly ask his father, "Don't you expect me to be what you made me, to live up to the things you taught me when I was a child, a teenager?"

His father would look at him with eyes bespeaking sadness and compassion. A picture of Birnbaum from that time, made by his son Menachem, has survived in the Birnbaum jubilee book,[2] published on his sixtieth birthday. It depicts him expressing wonderment and at the same time a steely resolve. Much as this boy revered his father, much as his father's prophet-like appearance was imprinted on his mind, he was not going to change completely as his two brothers had.

Uriel Birnbaum (1894–1956), the youngest of the three

sons, was a passionate soul, burning with intense fervor and a
love for his God that may have surprised even his father. He
had married a Catholic girl, the nurse who had taken care of
him after he lost both his legs during the First World War. This
noble young woman not only converted to Judaism but remained loyal to Uriel and her new faith to the very end,
throughout the Nazi period, including years of hiding from
the spying eyes of the Nazis.[3]

Uriel survived the Second World War together with his
family by hiding in Holland, with the help of the Dutch
underground. Naively, he believed that in the aftermath of the
war Austria would be restored to its old glory and once again
become a nation noted for tolerance, a model to all empires
whose populations comprised many ethnic minorities and
races.

Uriel's search for his God led him along a tortuous road.
Even after accepting all *mitzvot* (the Torah's commandments
and the oral traditions), he, a man of overwhelming devout-
ness, considered himself unworthy and his body too unholy to
place upon it the *tefillin*. This talented man devoted his art to
his religion. One selection of his *Gebete* ("Prayers"), printed in
the jubilee book, made an indelible impression on me. Praying
to his God, Uriel wrote:

> Lend me Your strength when I am weary,
> And weary I often am, uncontrollably. . . .

The following lines reveal his personal struggle in his attempts to reach his God.

> My God, how deep is the meaning of Your way,
> And how long are the roads leading to You. . . .

The calendar of the Agudath Israel of Vienna displayed an
impressive drawing depicting the young prophet Jeremiah
driven by an internal storm. The caption read:

And the Lord said to me:
"Do not say, I am still a boy,
But go wherever I send you
And speak whatever I command you.
Have no fear of them,
For I am with you to deliver you, declares the Lord."

(Jeremiah 1:7–8)

Uriel took this to be his task in life. Still, did he pick up his artificial legs to go out and, like his father, address his people? He *did* speak through his paintings and poems to those who visited his exhibitions and read his prayers. Yet, how powerless was this double amputee. He was overcome with a sense of insufficiency and frustration in the face of the lofty goals he aspired to on his long and winding road to his God.

It appears to be almost a miracle, in those days of fascination with socialism and rationalism, that Birnbaum's intelligent wife and two of his sons became deeply committed to the God of their husband and father.

NATHAN BIRNBAUM'S PROPHETIC MESSAGE

One year after Birnbaum's arrival in Holland from Berlin, his friends and admirers organized a mass meeting in honor of his seventieth birthday. This occasion proved to be the last time he spoke publicly to his people. His voice had lost its impressive resonance, but speaking with the majestic timbre and inflection of an elder sage, he was as convincing as ever.

He spoke about the state of the Jewish people being in mortal distress. Then, as if haunted by frightening premonitions, he concluded his message with a warning that his people should not rely on their influence in the international arena or the effect of a universal boycott of the German economy. Over and over he repeated the same phrase, until out of breath, "*Es wird aerger werden!*" ("Things will get worse, much worse, worse than you can imagine!").

He begged them to believe him because he had seen the boundless hatred in the eyes of the Nazis in Berlin. Birnbaum, the strong and courageous thinker, admitted that he had trembled, yes, actually trembled when perceiving the burning hatred and the rabid cruelty of their angry looks—angry merely because he existed! "Things will get worse, much worse!" A chilling silence fell over the audience in The Hague, then still a peaceful city in Holland.

The man of *teshuvah* who had called upon his people to reconsider and change their attitude then told them with deep sadness that the Jews, who as individuals are often smart and discerning, react in immature ways as a people. They lack the wisdom to recognize the senselessness of wild impulses and rash urges and exert political pressure by declaring a boycott against Germany, which would only make things worse. "And it will get worse! Much worse!" was the prophetic refrain of the final part of his address.

When this great visionary died two years later, the situation had indeed grown worse, much worse. In the two years that followed, things would deteriorate even further, and during the final years of that horrendous war the torment got indescribably worse.

Nathan Birnbaum, representing a unique form of *teshuvah*, paved the way for the thousands and perhaps tens of thousands who followed in his path. Unbendingly loyal to the truth, he did not seek God in order to provide for himself a niche in a corner of the world under God's protective wing. Instead, following in the footsteps of the prophets, he felt the call to broaden the scope of the shrunken divine presence. And in a world dominated by materialism and paganism, he intended to help by creating a niche for a Torah-based life of sanctity and purity.

II

THE PHENOMENON
OF *TESHUVAH*

6

PERSONAL RESPONSIBILITY

Repentance and forgiveness are divine gifts, as are the sinner's opportunity to bring sacrifices on the altar and to be forgiven. But the actual forgiveness engendered by an individual's sin offering is predicated on *teshuvah*. Sinners must confess their sins in order to be forgiven, as it is stated, "They shall confess the wrong that they have done" (Numbers 5:7).

But repentance applies not only to individual sinners. The Torah and the prophets quite explicitly demand collective repentance. And so it is stated in the Torah, "You shall return and obey the voice of the Lord your God" (Deuteronomy 30:8); and in the Prophets it is written, "Turn back, turn back from your evil ways—why should you die, O Family of Israel?" (Ezekiel 33:11); and "Return, O Israel, up to the Lord your God, for you have stumbled because of your sin" (Hosea 14:2).

The book of Jonah tells the dramatic case of an entire city returning to God in repentance. Jonah prophesied to the people of Nineveh, the capital of Assyria, that because of their wickedness their city would be destroyed within forty days.

When the people responded by repenting, fasting, and donning sackcloth, God accepted their *teshuvah* and rescinded His evil decree (Jonah 3:5–10).

Still, critical minds have always had doubts regarding repentance. Philosophers of old believed that an infinite Creator, of necessity, is detached from His finite creation. In their view, it is inconceivable that God, Who transcends time and space, can be affected by the acts and thoughts of temporal creatures. Such thinking negates any relationship between people and their Creator, denies the existence of *teshuvah*, and deprives people of a source for atonement—the God Who must accept their repentance.

It is true that modern thinkers have discarded these outdated concepts. But regardless of what the philosophers and theologians may propound, believers accept God as being unlimited and omnipotent and still accessible to His creatures (as opposed to the idea of a divinity detached from His creation by reasons of logic of an outdated epistemology).

DIVINE RECORDING

While the believer in Torah is fully prepared to ignore the reasonings and conclusions of the skeptics, he still faces some problems in his personal attempt to understand the dynamics of *teshuvah*.

A contemporary person, despite his faith, may still have some difficulty accepting the notion that separate files are kept in a heavenly filing system where minute-by-minute actions over the lifetime of billions of people are meticulously recorded. No wonder then, that many believers are perplexed by the unbelievable complexity of such a process of record keeping. This may be only a practical difficulty, but it causes many people to be concerned whether, in weighing the lives of billions of people, overlapping and interference could be avoided. They are fearful that the objectivity of personal judgment may become somewhat dubious. They therefore find it hard to accept personal responsibility for their deeds, repentance, or forgiveness. Yet, the Torah definitely expects man to repent, to offer specific sacrifices, and obtain forgiveness.

The Torah—both in its laws and its narrative parts—recognizes the personal accountability of the individual as well as the collective responsibility of a community. Even a Torah-observant Jew may not be able to resist the temptation to try to sort out what this means with regard to his understanding of divine judgment. Will repentance and forgiveness not seem to him to be unrealistic concepts?

KING DAVID'S DILEMMA

King David addresses this dilemma. In Psalm 19, noting that he is careful to keep the commandments of the Torah, he prays to God: "Who can be aware of *shegiyot* (errors)? Clear me of *nistarot* (acts that are hidden from me); keep your servant from *zeidim* (willful sins)" (Psalm19:12).

Lest we wonder why David included willful sins in his prayer, we find that he added the words, "*Al yimshelu vi*" ("Let them not overpower me"). It would not have made sense for him to ask God to help him from sinning willfully and wittingly; as a man of free will, he needed to accomplish this on his own. But what he asked God was to save him from becoming addicted to sin.

He concluded with joyful confidence and faith: "Then," if God will make me understand the unwitting sins and cleanse me from the things that are hidden, acts I am unaware of, and from addictions to sin, "then I shall be blameless and clear of *pesha rav* (rebellious transgression)" (Psalm 19:13–14).

What was the source of David's optimism? Perhaps he

intuitively understood the message Isaiah would convey centuries later to all evildoers: "Let the wicked give up his way, the sinful man his plans; let him turn back to the Lord, *virachameihu* (and He will show him mercy) *ki yarbeh lislo'ach* (for He will never tire of forgiving him)" (Isaiah 55:7).

In the term *virachameihu* (and He will show him mercy) we sense God's compassion toward any repentant who needs divine assistance. Even when a sinner is unable to grasp the full significance of his misdeeds, God apparently assists him by filling in the gap in the awareness of his transgression.

It is this assurance of God's compassionate help that led David to conclude his psalm by declaring confidently, "Then I shall be blameless and clear of rebellious transgression."

In summary, the Torah–observant Jew believes with unquestioning faith in the existence of a comprehensive divine record of his personal conduct. His problem is how to gain access to this account of his deeds so that he may become aware of the acts he is expected to regret. Furthermore, he is at a loss to understand the hopes and thoughts that impelled his actions, unable to absorb and assimilate the innumerable bits and pieces of insights he received by intuition and by the grace of God, responding to his prayers. But he does believe in God's promise of special compassion with the repentant sinner.

This inadequacy to properly define his failures finds expression in the preamble to the recitation of the *Viduy*, the confession of Yom Kippur in which the penitent, wondering what to say to God, Who is omniscient, addresses the Creator:

> You know the secrets of the universe, and the hiddenmost mysteries of all the living. You probe all innermost chambers of my body and test thoughts and emotions. Nothing is hidden from You and nothing is concealed from Your eyes.

He then asks:

May it be Your will that You forgive us for all our errors (*chatoteinu*), and You pardon us for all our iniquities (*avonoteinu*), and You atone for us for all our willful sins (*pesha'einu*).

But even after realizing that a celestial record does exist, one may still wonder what relevance the existence of this record of one's deeds has for the despondent confessant on earth. Is he supposed to take a giant leap to Heaven above in order to get a glimpse at the total printout of all his good and bad deeds?

For the answer, let us look at Jacob's dream of the cosmic ladder. While he was resting at the bottom of the ladder, Jacob saw heavenly messengers carrying upward the bits of his fragmented and troubled existence in Canaan. He also perceived other angels descending from Heaven, symbolically carrying the package of his future in the foreign environment of Laban's home.

The aggadic source puts it beautifully: When Jacob awoke he noticed that the stones he had placed around himself for protection against predators had been fused into one large stone (Rashi, Genesis 28:11).

Like Jacob, man on earth need not actually climb to the higher spheres. He can lie down on the solid earth, gaze upward all the way to the *Kissei Hakavod* (the divine throne), and absorb the radiant light of descending messengers who offer him a gift of an integrated, meaningful, future life's image. Now, like the stones framing Jacob's bed, the separate and discordant pieces in any man's life can come together to form an integrated whole.

THE MODEL

The average repentant is unable to integrate the diverse pieces of his life by himself. He knows that God's ways are deep and the final goal is remote. He cannot decipher God's words and the divine messages He sends through His angels. The repentant must want to be able to form a mental picture of himself and visualize the divine record of his good deeds and failings. But is this not wishful thinking, an unrealistic and farfetched idea?

The truth is, were man able to climb the cosmic ladder and be provided with the innumerable data that make up his thoughts and deeds, he might be able to integrate these facts and figures and fit them into a rational mosaic. It follows that the concept of a divine record of man's life is not a suprarational phenomenon. It merely cannot be imagined and expressed in common-sense language.

The Torah itself offers an approach to enable the thinking man to comprehend esoteric philosophical concepts. We find countless examples of such conceptual models in the aggadic, midrashic, and kabbalistic literature. The parables and allegories contained in these works afford man the opportunity to express profound ideas in terms that make sense to corporeal man.

THINKING IN DEPTH

Chasidim and the followers of Rabbi Yisrael Salanter's ethical *Mussar* movement regarded nature as a form of divine revelation. To start with, they immensely enjoyed the wonders of God's universe. At each season of the year, at any time of the day, they would behold with surprise and wonderment a world that they perceived as a harmonious symphony composed by the Creator. Their eyes and ears might see in nature a manifestation of awesome divine acts. The graceful flight of a bird or the fragrance of a blooming flower and the intricate functioning of the human body would evoke an admiring whisper: "*Niflaot HaBoreh!*" ("What marvelous acts of the Creator these are!").

Still, even among *chasidim* and mussarists, who were deeply in awe of God's creation, there were many who hesitated to explore the mysteries of divine "wondrous acts." They preferred to follow the admonition: *"Bemuflah mimecha al tidrosh"* ("Do not search for the meaning of that which is remote and hidden from you") (*Chagigah* 13a).

The majority of people of faith, however, believe that being a creature of God endowed with a divine spark, it is a Jew's duty at least to attempt to understand God's ways to the extent that they are not "hidden." They feel bolstered by the Torah itself, which does not hesitate to introduce symbols, allegories, and metaphors that render intelligible to the average person not only miraculous manifestations of divine guidance but even general truths that man would not have been able to discover by himself. Not everything that appears remote and concealed is, in fact, inaccessible to human understanding.

One of the well-known symbols of this genre is the ladder in Jacob's dream, standing on the ground and reaching up toward Heaven (Genesis 28:12). Commentators like Rabbi Yitzchak Arama, in his book *Akeidat Yitzchak*[1] view this ladder as an allegory—or rather as a *mashal*, a model—illustrating how man's deeds and prayers reach up all the way to Heaven. Thus, the Torah uses an allegory to explain communication between man and God.

Another device often employed in the Torah is anthropomorphism, whereby human forms or characteristics are ascribed to Divinity. The psalmist, for example, endows God with human attributes, using simple words to express fundamental articles of faith. He uses this literary tool to explain the idea of *hashgachah peratit* (divine providence) for each and every individual, an idea that has baffled thinkers of all generations. In plain everyday language, speaking of God in human terms, the psalmist declares, "From Heaven God looks down; He sees all mankind. From His dwelling place He oversees all inhabitants of earth" (Psalm 33:13–14).

AGGADAH, THE KEY TO UNDERSTANDING

Additionally, convincing justification for in-depth probing to understand the ways of God can be found in the famous talmudic suggestion that if you wish to come close to and understand "*et mi she'amar vehayah ha'olam*" ("the One who spoke and the world came into being"), turn to the world of the *Aggadah*. The aggadic method of parable, allegory, and metaphor provides answers to the searching questions by the way it interprets such passages as "*Sod Hashem lirei'av*" ("The secret of God is for those who fear Him, to them He makes known His covenant") (Psalm 25:14). *Sod*, according to the *Aggadah*, signifies secret (kabbalistic) wisdom. God thus made a covenant to impart the understanding of His mysteries to those worthy of this knowledge.

Interestingly, we may find additional hints of God's eagerness for man to discover His secrets in a fascinating interpretation of the biblical passage, "*Zecher assah lenifle'otav, chanun verachum Hashem*" ("He created a record of His wonders; the Lord is gracious and full of compassion") (Psalm 111:4).

Issar Mazel[2] interprets this passage to mean that God, in His compassion for those who are God-fearing and thirsting for knowledge and understanding, created a *zecher* consisting of intelligible patterns and legible records of His awe-inspiring acts. *Zecher* refers to the fact that the Creator provides, to the man seeking to understand the world, actual bits of the blueprints He used in creating the universe.

THE *MASHAL* AS A MODEL

The device the aggadist uses to make abstract concepts accessible to people is the *mashal*, the parable-style model. He frequently introduces an explanatory discussion with the words "*Emshol lecha mashal, lemah hadavar domeh*" ("Let me give you a *mashal*, an allegory, a metaphor that actually is a model to which you can compare the concept I am presenting to you"). He then creates suitable models that offer formal likenesses and analogies, thereby simplifying the understanding of the phenomenon under discussion. The aggadic model is extremely helpful in gaining a clear understanding of *teshuvah* and forgiveness.

THE *TEDA* MODEL

Teda is one of the lesser-known rabbinic models; its literal translation is "You will know." It is generally used in the following context: "Observe the world around you (*teda*); there you will find a *mashal* that will answer your problem." It is a model of special interest to the study of personal providence because of its directness and simplicity. It is used in the aggadic literature to prove the plausibility of apparent exaggerations, such as the rabbinic statement, "In the distant future, all women will bear a child every day of their lives" (*Shabbat* 30b). The aggadist, realizing that such a degree of fertility staggers credulity, advises his audience, "*Teda*"— "Look at the animal world, where chickens lay eggs every day."[3]

The talmudic sage does not really prove his statement. By using the *teda* method, he has only demonstrated that his suggestion of incredible fecundity is not an impossible phenomenon.

It is true that the aggadists and kabbalists, who plumb the depths of Torah wisdom and boldly scale the heights of mystical understanding, feel forced to go even further. It should come as no surprise that they created a variety of models of their own in order to give substance to their esoteric notions. These are "extended *teda* models."

The analogies aggadists and kabbalists use in building these models are not limited to simple objects like a tangible egg or a special kind of tree. To create analogies for their ideas, they draw also on the natural sciences, regardless of whether they relate to tangible or intangible features of theories of natural law.

The question may now arise as to whether the basic character of the *teda* model changes if we extend it to the realm of the immaterial and spiritual. The answer is that the extended *teda* model does not change its relation to reality, provided it limits itself to the use of features of nature actually functioning in the observable world. It merely has the increased potential of simplifying the understanding of the abstract concepts aggadists and kabbalists are dealing with in their philosophy of the universe.

The most famous example of an extended *teda* model is the kabbalistic representation of the divine attributes. These are known as the ten *sefirot*, the spheres or vessels through which the light of the Creator emanates from the realm of the highest level down to man's low level of the physical world. These attributes are grouped in three triangles, the corners of which are arranged so that the divine attributes of unlimited flow of love are situated on a vertical line connecting the corners on the right; their opposites, the limiting attributes, are on a vertical line connecting the left corners, while the attributes of merger (of reality) are aligned on a vertical line in between the right and the left corners.

A MODEL OF ACCOUNTABILITY

After this preliminary inquiry into the usage of the model in the Torah, the Prophets, aggadic literature, and kabbalistic literature, we venture to follow their example in attempting to create adequate models that will simplify the understanding of

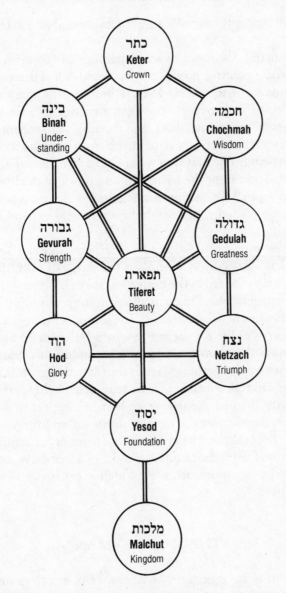

Illustration from *Pardes Rimonim*, Gate of the *Tzinorot* (Conduits). Representation of the Spiritual *Sefirot* (Emanations).

the basic concepts of man's accountability and divine forgiveness.

Since man is the focus of accountability and forgiveness, an appropriate existing model for man and his relationship to God must be discovered. Man is indeed a unique creature composed of an extremely complex structure of atoms, cells, nerve tissue, mental faculties, and spiritual components. One could begin, therefore, by structuring from scratch a model for a human being. The first step would be to visualize what image might best represent the basic building block of the body, the complex atom.[4] As a simplified model for the atom we envision a huge pulsating soap bubble, alternately expanding and contracting.

For the more sophisticated reader one might suggest a model that more closely resembles the image of man, that of a gigantic ship moored in the boundless sea of life energy, which fills the entire world. This is in line with the psalmist's passage, "*chesed Hashem malah haaretz*" ("The unbounded divine nourishing forces of life fill the entire world") (Psalm 33:5).

But now the problem arises: What holds this huge soap bubble or vessel together? What is the force that gives it lasting stability? On reflection, is not the atom itself held together by the gravity field of the universe? Is it not logical to assume, therefore, that just as the minuscule atoms and the vast universe are held together by the immense force of cohesion of the gravitational field, the complex model of a human is also held together by an inner affinity, which we usually define as personality?

THE MODEL—MAN

Man, who is an aggregate of atoms, cells, nerve tissue, and mental and spiritual elements, appears as a complex of masses of energy possessing a vibrational structure. To put it more simply, each person has a range of "wave lengths" that is uniquely his own. By using the human body as a model, one discovers fascinating features with which one can understand elements of faith in model terms of natural phenomena.

Space is saturated with an infinite number of different wave frequencies representing different radio stations. Yet, notwithstanding the overabundance of wave lengths, one is able to tune in the *one* frequency he desires. He finds that the signals of the station he has selected are virtually free of interference from the numerous other frequencies, proof positive that vibrational structures do not overlap or intrude on each other.

SEPARABILITY

Our *teda* model suggests that man, who is essentially a vibrational structure, has an extremely sensitive tuning capability. He has the capacity, by means of an inner antenna, to select a desired wavelength on which to receive life energies flowing from his surrounding worldfield to his individual "ship."

On a more down-to-earth level, one might say that every individual is unique in body and soul. As our sages aptly put it, "Just as no two faces look alike, no two minds think alike" (Jerusalem Talmud, *Berachot* 89).

In the world, no one is ever displaced or interfered with by even a hairbreadth. Thus in God's ledger there is no disorder, overlapping, or intermingling between the record of one individual and the billions of others coexisting in the world. Man's individuality is guaranteed and *hashgachah peratit* (personal divine providence), instead of being an unrealistic article of faith, is an inherent feature in all creatures.

To summarize, since the ability of a person to do *teshuvah* is bound up with his accountability to God, it is contingent on the uniqueness of the individual. Our vibrational model establishes the privacy, separateness, and individuality of each person. No man can drown out, not even for an instant, another person's identity. Each individual is wholly responsible for his actions. Thus, the *teda* model of vibrational structure successfully simplifies the understanding of the fundamental principle of *hashgachah peratit*. Since, according to nature, the record of one person's deeds is never confused with that of another, a person's distinguishableness is not subject to question any longer. On the contrary, it is a phenomenon based on empirically valid natural law.

7

Two Ways of Repentance

Our tradition recognizes two main reasons that impel a person to do *teshuvah*: the basic *teshuvah miyirah* (repentance motivated by fear) and the lofty *teshuvah mei'ahavah* (repentance motivated by love).

Since fear of divine punishment is a universal trait that is ingrained in the human soul, all repentance begins with fear. Having taken the initial step of repenting out of fear, the penitent ideally—but not necessarily—progresses to the higher stage of repentance, *teshuvah* out of love of God. Only in rare instances is an individual inspired to repent via the direct route of pure love of God, passing over the stage of repentance out of fear.

Our sages offer illuminating insights into these two facets of repentance. They assure a sinner who repents out of fear that all his *zedonot* (purposeful transgressions), will be transformed into *shegagot* (unintentional sinful acts). When the sinner's *teshuvah* is prompted by love of God, however, even his willful transgressions become *zechuyot* (actual merits) that are credited to his heavenly account as good deeds.[1]

REPENTANCE OUT OF FEAR

Repentance out of fear begins when a person decides one day that he wants to return to God because terrible things are happening to him. Perhaps he is overcome by health problems, family troubles, or grave financial problems. He knew all along that many of his acts were contrary to the laws of the Torah, but only now, in the wake of his personal hardships, he has become concerned about the punishment for his transgressions. In fact, he may be convinced that if he had realized the seriousness of his sin initially, he would not have transgressed willingly in the first place.

The question arises as to whether this person's sin should be considered a deliberate transgression, since at the time he did the sin he was oblivious to the seriousness of its consequences.

Torah law stipulates that a violator of the law cannot be punished unless he has been cautioned beforehand that his act is forbidden and that such a transgression is punishable by such and such a penalty. If he has received no such warning, his transgression cannot be prosecuted in a Jewish court of law (although, of course, he is held accountable for his act before the heavenly tribunal).

And so, a sinner who does *teshuvah after* realizing the full extent of the consequences of his sinful act indicates that he would not have committed the sin had he intellectually and emotionally understood its many ramifications and repercussions.

Clearly, such a deliberate sinner can be considered a *shogeg*, an unwitting transgressor, one who has not been fully apprised of the seriousness of his sin.

REPENTANCE OUT OF LOVE

The rabbis tell us that God takes all the intentional transgressions of a *baal teshuvah* who is motivated by *ahavah* (love of

God and His Torah) and transforms them into *zechuyot* (merits), indeed into *mitzvot*. Why is this so? How are we to understand this?

Repentance out of love results from a complete change of heart, mind, and soul. The sinner has become a person who is starting life anew by making a strong commitment to God. This radical change comes about if a person who has committed many sins realizes how far removed from God he has become. This sense of estrangement makes him feel ashamed. He asks himself, "How could I have been blind to the goodness of God, Who keeps me alive and sustains me?" The sinner's shame brings on regret and a frightening feeling of loneliness and isolation that traumatizes his total personality. Shaken to the core, he restructures his life and his relationship to his God. While the basic personality of a penitent who repents out of fear remains unchanged, a penitent who repents out of love is reborn with a deep yearning to be closer to God.

It is this yearning that the Torah has in mind when it states, "Love God your Lord with *all* your heart" ("*bechol levavecha*") (Deuteronomy 6:5). The sages, noting that *levavecha* is written with a double *beit* (instead of a single *beit—libecha*), suggest that we must love God with the totality of our heart, with both our inclinations—the *yetzer hatov* (our good impulse) and the *yetzer hara* (our evil impulse).

We find a prime example of such love of God in David, the prototype of the *baal teshuvah*-for-love who felt an insatiable longing for God, which he expressed with words of unequalled emotion: "*Tzamah lechah nafshi*" ("My soul thirsts for You") (Psalm 63:2). His feeling of spiritual longing for the nearness of God is followed by the words, "*Kamah lecha besari*" ("My *body* yearns for You"), a phrase that includes within his yearning for God even his bodily senses, which one is inclined to associate with the *yetzer hara*, the physical urge in man.

In this moving verse David is telling God that he, the *baal teshuvah*-for-love, in rededicating his life, has subdued his physical drive and integrated it with his spiritual longings.

A *BAAL TESHUVAH* RANKS
HIGHER THAN A *TZADDIK*

In talmudic literature, the *baal teshuvah*-out-of-love is treated with a high degree of respect and admiration and occupies a lofty position bordering on saintliness. And so we read in the *Gemara*, "*Bemakom shebaalei teshuvah omedim ein tzaddikim gemurim yecholim laamod*" ("In the place occupied by a *baal teshuvah*, not even an accomplished *tzaddik* [a totally righteous person] can stand") (*Berachot* 34b).

At first glance this seems incongruous, but we must realize that in the soul of an ideal *baal teshuvah*, one who repented out of love, all memories of past rebellious acts are consumed in a blazing fire of longing for God's nearness, a closeness he had missed for so long. Obviously, the more a sinner has erred, the more powerful his sense of shame and the stronger his urge to reshape his life and fill it with the values he neglected during the years of his estrangement, so that each purposeful sin of the past turns into a *zechut*, a source of spiritual elevation. Thus, by repenting, the *baal teshuvah* accumulates a wealth of *mitzvot* that he performs with sincerity and unusual depth. No wonder he held in such high esteem.

Still, why does a *baal teshuvah*, meritorious though he is, rate higher than a *tzaddik gamur*, a totally righteous man? Should not a *tzaddik* be accorded at least the same high regard as a *baal teshuvah*? It is difficult to accept the idea that a *tzaddik* who has lived a pristine life, removed from sin and temptation, does not measure up to a former sinner.

A *tzaddik* has never experienced the overwhelming sense of shame a willful sinner feels. He has never suffered the loneliness and remoteness from his God a sinner endures. He therefore does not experience the *baal teshuvah*'s overpowering urge to make amends. It is this impetus, this relentless drive to do better and reach higher, that places the *baal teshuvah*-out-of-love on a higher plateau than the *tzaddik gamur*, the perfect righteous man.

But we ask, is all this not merely a theoretical discourse? Does a *baal teshuvah*-out-of-love-of-God actually exist? Indeed he does. There are people who for many years have been estranged from God, believing that the infinite God is too remote from mundane affairs to be affected by and react to man's conduct. The psalmist aptly characterizes such unbelievers and agnostics, stating, "They think, 'God does not see it, the God of Jacob does not pay heed' " (Psalm 94:7).

Then, one day, perhaps driven by the loneliness of his existence, or possibly because of convincing arguments, an individual discovers that he has been wrong, that his Creator is not distant, unseeing, and undiscerning. He realizes that, quite the contrary, God is close to man and aware of all his doings.

It is true that an ideal repentant, a person who suddenly, in a bright flash, recognizes the truth, is extremely rare. But there are others—and they are not rare at all—who are touched by the newness of their experience of their Creator and who gradually gain further understanding and insight. They are not easily recognized because their experience often does not arrive with suddenness and great intensity. But these people, too, are repentants out of love, and today they are returning to Torah in a mighty stream.

Usually only a person who takes a sincere interest in his fellow man and especially in people who in the past have strayed, intuitively recognizes the many who lost God and found Him again in a gradual and natural process. Both the rare "instant *baal teshuvah*" and the more prevalent "gradual *baal teshuvah*" have found the way to *teshuvah mei'ahavah*, repentance out of love, in a great journey of discovery.

ECHETA VE'ASHUV—I WILL SIN AND REPENT

There are exceptions to every rule, and even a concept as lofty as *teshuvah* out of love is qualified by certain conditions.

A well-known *Mishnah* states that a person who says, "*Echeta ve'ashuv, echeta ve'ashuv*" ("I will sin and repent; I will sin and repent again"), intending to remain a habitual sinner, believing that in the end he will become a *baal teshuvah*, "*ein maspikin beyado laasot teshuvah*" ("will not be given an opportunity to repent") (*Yoma* 8:9).

We must assume that this sinner is sincere in wanting to repent each time he sinned, yet the *Mishnah* tells us that it simply will not work. Obviously, this is not intended as a punishment for attempting to misuse the option of *teshuvah*. Rather, by saying "*Echeta ve'ashuv*," such a would-be "repentant sinner" is indicating that he has misunderstood the true nature of repentance. *Ashuv* (I will repent) implies shame, regret, and a change of heart. For a *baal teshuvah*-out-of-love to plan to sin and repent and then to sin and repent again would be paradoxical. How could a person before committing a sin consider that afterwards he will be devastated by *genuine* shame and contrition, and still at the same time contemplate to sin again? It is inconceivable that he would imagine that after his first repentance he would sin again and still be overcome by feelings of guilt caused by this repetition of his rebellious act.

Clearly, by resolving in advance to sin and to repent again and again, he has negated the basic principle of *teshuvah*. Of course, he does indeed fully comprehend the meaning of *teshuvah*. Mindlessly, he may have thought of *teshuvah* as a mechanical device that somehow is capable of erasing a sin, no matter how often it is repeated. Regrettably, when it is too late he will find out that his brand of *teshuvah* is ineffective since it is nothing more than play-acting and self-deception, lacking the essential change of heart and mind.

Some sinners may mistakenly bolster their erroneous view of *teshuvah* as a mechanical device by pointing to a talmudic opinion that states that Yom Kippur brings about automatic removal of sins, even for sinners who show no regret and do not repent. But even according to this opinion, it is inherent in the exceptional character of Yom Kippur, the Day of Atonement per se (*itzumo shel yom*), that forgiveness is granted without prior genuine *teshuvah*.

Throughout Jewish history the unique divine gift of *teshuvah* has been distorted and misunderstood by many as being a purely mechanical device. The prophet Isaiah, along with all the early prophets, fulminated against this travesty. He denounced those evildoers who with bloodstained hands brought fat animals as sacrifices, in the belief that these were instruments for obtaining atonement for sin and freedom from punishment (Isaiah 1:10–15). Their repentance—if it existed at all—lacked any trace of shame and regret. When *teshuvah* becomes a token gesture and mere lip service without a change of heart, it cannot create the momentum that causes a sinner to mend his ways.

Chasidic literature relates that a great chasidic *rebbe*, revealing his magnanimity to any type of sinner, interpreted the *Mishnah* in *Yoma* regarding the person who intends "to sin and repent, sin and repent" in a way that completely reverses its plain meaning. Focusing on the phrase *ein maspikin beyado laasot teshuvah*, the chasidic *rebbe* considered the term *maspikin* as being derived from *safek*, doubt. The resultant new meaning is, "If a person says, 'I will sin and repent, sin and repent,' *there is no doubt* that he *can* do *teshuvah* should he decide to do so."

Apparently, the chasidic *rebbe* is saying that if a person plans to "sin and repent" over and over again and this person ultimately decides to do genuine *teshuvah*, then nothing can prevent him from doing so. However, since he has made a mockery of *teshuvah* by making it a habit to sin and repent, he will be deprived of the divine assistance that a genuine *baal teshuvah* is granted. The chasidic *rebbe*, however, holds out a ray of hope for such a sinner who initially wanted to outsmart God but who is now ready for such a rare, sincere *teshuvah*.

A person who declares "I will sin and repent, and I will sin and repent again" demonstrates, despite his nonchalant attitude, a deep-seated faith in the necessity of repentance for any sin he commits. Evidently, he would not consider sinning if he did not harbor the mistaken belief that he could repent for such premeditated sins. Not for a moment did he contemplate sinning—"*Echeta*" ("I will sin")—without linking his sin to "*ve'ashuv*" ("and I will repent"). His frame of reference is fundamentally different from that of the cynical evildoers in the days of Isaiah who offered fat animals to be burned on the altar without repenting or feeling the slightest remorse. By contrast, the "*echeta ve'ashuv*" type of sinner, while believing in the need for *teshuvah*, is only confused in his understanding of the spiritual and mental forces that generate *teshuvah*. In the chasidic view, this deep-seated belief in the need for *teshuvah* is a redeeming quality that offers the hope that his *teshuvah* will be accepted. After all, he is basically no different from a person who sinned in error. And even though he had put *teshuvah* out of reach by declaring, "I will sin and repent," the power of genuine repentance is boundless and can overcome even this formidable barrier.

The phenomenon of habitual sinning and repenting is essentially an extreme form of *iruv*, of confusion and muddled thinking, for the "*echeta ve'ashuv*" type of sinner does not realize that his deep belief in the necessity of *teshuvah* causes the door to *teshuvah* to be closed to him. If he at last understands that he has sinned against the very gift of *teshuvah*, he may be overcome by shame and remorse. Conscience-stricken, he may then take a giant leap to enter the *shaarei teshuvah*, the gates of repentance. He must realize, though, that he is taking this leap all by himself, an irrational act outside the framework of the divine gift, and therefore without divine assistance. Having mustered the courage to turn his back on his regrettable past, he will find the gates of repentance open to receive him and offer him access to the nearness of God, Who may also include him in His abundant measure of forgiveness.

8
FORGIVENESS AND DIVINE
DATA GATHERING

Modern technology provides the scientist with advanced tools for gathering scientific, statistical, and historical data, even data relating to mental processes. In recent decades supercomputers have been developed that are capable of storing, collating, and integrating immense amounts of information. It is conceivable that in the not-too-distant future all data concerning the location, function, and accomplishments of any given individual anywhere in the world will be registered automatically in the brain of such an ingeniously engineered supercomputer.

Such a supercomputer may serve as a model for *hashgachah peratit* to help us understand that "God, looking down from Heaven, sees all mankind" (Psalm 33:13) and creates and maintains a personal account for each individual.[1]

The computer is providing us with a faint echo of the Creator's *Sefer Hazichronot*, His "Book of Remembrances," which contains the record of everyone's deeds.

FORGIVENESS AND THE *KISSEI HAKAVOD*

The Creator, in His great compassion, provided us with a *zecher*, a pattern in nature that enables us to understand His ways. In addition to revealing Himself through nature, God also revealed in the Torah, and later through His prophets, basic models by means of which we can form mental images of the seemingly contradictory, abstract idea of divine providence for the individual.

The psalmist whom we quoted before speaks of two models of heavenly observation, centers where all data regarding a person's conduct are gathered: *shamayim*, the "heavens"; and *mechon shivto*, "His dwelling place." He states, "God looks down from Heaven; He sees all mankind; from His dwelling place He oversees all inhabitants of earth" (Psalm 33:13-14).

"Heaven," the divine throne, can be viewed as a model for the general observation post, where God is looking down from a distance, supervising the totality of nature and the functioning of its God-given laws (*hashgachah kelalit*), whereas "His dwelling place" can be viewed as the Temple, representing a model for a specialized guidance center for close supervision, geared to keeping track of the actions of each individual (*hashgachah peratit*).

This brings us to the point of discussing the *Kissei Hakavod*, the heavenly throne. Initially, we hesitated to extend the use of the *teda* model to this lofty and esoteric subject for fear of demeaning the *kedushah* (sanctity) and *sod* (mystery) attached to it. But it was decided to follow the precedent set by the Torah and the prophets Isaiah and Ezekiel, who used the *mashal* and the approach of the *teda* model to bring the function of the *Kissei* closer to our level of understanding.

In his prophecy, Isaiah is shown a vision of the divine throne reaching down to earth. Describing his vision he says, "I beheld God seated on a high and lofty throne; and its lower edge filled the Temple" (Isaiah 6:1).

The added detail of the throne's lower edge filling the Temple suggests that the function of the divine throne is intimately connected with events on earth. Isaiah explains that the *shulav*, the lower edge of the throne, was draped like a bridal gown over the *heichal*, the court of the Sanctuary, the site of the altar. This imagery alludes to the close link that exists between the throne and the people's sacrifices, through which they obtain forgiveness for their sins.

In Isaiah's last prophecy he again spoke of the heavenly throne, proclaiming, "*Hashamayim Kissi*" ("The Heaven is My throne and the earth is My footstool") (Isaiah 66:1).

The phrase, "The earth is My footstool," implies that the earth in its entirety—not just the Temple court or the Sanc-tuary—serves as God's footstool, symbolizing God's total control of the world.[2]

Nevertheless, in examining the text of the prophetic de-scription of the *kissei* we detect a number of details that seem to be contradictory. On the one hand, the lower edge of the throne filling the Temple court clearly indicates that God's attention is focused on man and his world. By contrast, the adjectives "high" and "lofty," used to describe the throne, point in the opposite direction, suggesting the *kissei* to be detached from earth and belonging entirely to the spiritual realm. But then again, the prophet sees God also as involved with the earth, seated on His throne like a king, the sovereign ruler and supreme judge of the world, surrounded by angels who carry out God's commands to the minutest detail here on earth.

Despite the seeming inconsistencies, there can be no doubt that the *kissei* is meant to be viewed in a dual role, representing the infinite God's sovereignty over the world of Heaven above as well as His dominion over the finite world.

The prophet uses the image of the throne as a model to make the concept of God's rule of the world comprehensible and imaginable to finite man. He depicts the Creator's throne as an

ordinary royal throne and without hesitation describes its
lower edge as filling the Temple court. The most surprising
aspect of the prophet's message is that, in conveying his
model, he depicts the Creator, Who transcends any shape,
form, or image, as being seated on that throne like a flesh-
and-blood monarch.

The prophet is presenting a profound mystical experience in
p'shat form, that is, in human terms, making it intelligible to
everyone. In the same way, the *p'shat* approach has also been
used in translating the prophet's imagery into the language of
modern-day man. By using the terminology of today—vibrational structure, data bank, computer printout, and the like—
we do not in the least diminish the saintly character of Isaiah's
throne.[3]

On the contrary, God oversees and judges man and His
judgment is not predicated solely on His omniscience, but
rather on the record every man writes with his own deeds.
God in His abundant compassion has supplied us with the
tools that enable us to get at least a vague idea of God's ways.

THE HEAVENLY SUPERCOMPUTER

There exists an intimate connection between the *Kissei* and the
Sanctuary of the *Bet Hamikdash* in Jerusalem. To put it very
plainly, the *Kissei* reminds us of a center controlling the two-
way traffic in the universal God–man relationship of sacrifices
rising up from the Sanctuary and divine forgiveness flowing
down from above.[4] Using the *teda* model of the supercomputer, we might characterize forgiveness as the "delete key"
on a word processor, which, when pressed, instantly erases an
entire page or an entire document. Similarly, divine forgiveness irretrievably wipes away sin, as it says, "I wipe away your
sins like a cloud, your transgression like mist" (Isaiah 44:22).
Despite its simplicity, our model does not remove all diffi-

culties in interpreting the communication between the *Kissei* and each individual on earth. Do confusion and overlapping occur when God considers the individual accounts of billions of people? Isn't there a danger of good and bad deeds being credited or charged to the wrong account?

As we have seen, such fears are entirely unfounded. The *separability* of the vibrational structure that serves as a model for man's personality guarantees full privacy and accuracy in the reception of each individual record. Consequently, no two records can ever be mixed up.

There is also the problem of the instability of the imprints. Can we really visualize in the *teda* way that the fragile and delicate data of our records could survive the rigors of being transferred to the assumedly space-wise remote celestial center of accountability? Will the imprints arrive at their heavenly destination without distortion or mutilation? Although at first glance this may seem to present a serious challenge, the laws of nature actually support the application of the *teda* model in this case. Even if we were to assume that our life's imprints had to travel great distances to reach the realm of the *Kissei*, such physical, mental, and spiritual forms of energy are virtually indestructible. Recent experiments prove that a signal that is beamed toward a heavenly body in outer space arrives there intact and is bounced back to earth without the slightest damage. This certainly tends to lend additional support to the validity of using the *teda* model with respect to the *Kissei*.

In this connection, it is interesting to note that more than half a century ago, Sir Stanley Eddington, a well-known British mathematician and astrophysicist, described the permanence of records. He suggested that an observer on a cosmic platform situated about four thousand light years from earth would be able to see Abraham climbing Mount Moriah to sacrifice his son Isaac, since it took the light rays recording this event about four thousand years to reach his distant space platform. The signals of any event occurring on earth will continue to radiate through space. By the same token, a record of all our actions—whether important or trivial—remains forever intact.

MENTAL AND SPIRITUAL IMPRINTS

Does this permanent retention of our records also include imprints of emotional and spiritual experience? While it is true that spiritual and emotional experiences seemingly lack tangibility, they are, nevertheless, real sensations and conscious feelings that markedly affect man's life and that of his fellow man.

In the aggadic view, the prayers that emanate from a person's heart and are uttered by his lips are carried aloft by the *po'alei tefillot*, the angels who bring up prayers, all the way to the *Kissei Hakavod*. Moreover, talmudic sources state, "*Gedolah teshuvah shemagaat ad Kissei Hakavod*" ("The feelings of regret, shame, and repentance reach the lofty heights of the *Kissei Hakavod*"). Should such powerful and far-reaching emotions be considered less real and less tangible than the images of casual acts in a person's daily life?

The imprint of any event, anywhere in the universe, is preserved. The comprehensive record of a person's deeds—good and bad—including his spiritual and intellectual accomplishments, is stored within the memory of the *Kissei Hakavod*, the counterpart of a universal data bank. Thus no deed is ever lost or misplaced.

The *kissei* is described in its full glory in the prayers of Rosh Hashanah, the day whose focus is on the Creator's *Sefer Hazichronot*, the book containing the totality of all records. In a prayer radiating with faith we state, "*Zecher kol hayetzur*" ("The record of all that You have created reaches Your Throne")—man's acts and his assignments, his intentions and thoughts—all of them, "*lefanecha ba*" ("appear before Your Throne on this day of accounting for every creature").

9

INSTANT *TESHUVAH*

Adam, Cain, and David, the prototypes of repentant sinners, all had one feature in common: after their repentance, each was given the opportunity to build a new life. But not every repentant sinner fits this pattern. There are many sinners who do not repent until they have reached an advanced age; some do *teshuvah* only when they are in the throes of death. For indeed, it is never too late to repent: "Until the day of his death You await him; if he repents, You accept him immediately" (*Mussaf* for the High Holy Days). Of course, people who repent only at the end of their days do not have the opportunity to create a new Torah-observant life.

The question arises as to how such instant *teshuvah* is acceptable. How can an individual attain eternal bliss without having built, after his repentance, a reservoir of good deeds, love of God, and love of the Torah?

The *Gemara* in *Avodah Zarah* (17a) relates a story that focuses on this problem. Eliezer ben Doradya, a notorious sinner who had violated every law of ethics and morality, came to realize one day the futility of his way of life and the abomination he

119

had made of it. The story of this instant *teshuvah* as told in the *Gemara* is fascinating in the depth of its symbolism and its conceptual breadth. We are told that the last woman he had been with, a courtesan who demanded a high price for her favors, accidentally emitted an offensive odor. Deeply embarrassed, she told Eliezer that just as she was unable to prevent gas from emerging from her body and undo what she had done, so would he not be able to return to his God and Torah law. Deeply shocked, Eliezer tried to find a way to *teshuvah*. Appealing for help, he asked, in succession, the mountains, the sun, and the moon to intervene on his behalf. They turned him down, pointing to their own frailty and the immutability of their existence. He concluded that *teshuvah* depended on himself and himself alone.

Deeply remorseful, he climbed to the top of a hill, sat down on a rock, and, totally dejected, placed his head between his knees, bemoaning his wasted life. Since in his contorted position his body was severely cramped and his lungs were deprived of oxygen, his soul left his body. Suprisingly, a heavenly voice was heard declaring that the sinner had gained admission to *Olam Haba* (the World-to-Come).

How are we to understand the acceptance of this sinner's deathbed *teshuvah*? Here is a person who departed this world without having accumulated a storehouse of good deeds. He certainly had no admirable character traits to present to the heavenly tribunal. How will a person who is totally lacking in piety and benevolence be able to adapt to the holy atmosphere of the spiritual World-to-Come? This story seems to challenge our understanding that *teshuvah* is a rejuvenation of a person by means of which one can build a new and restructured life.

The premise of the story of repentance at life's end, which has the power to open the gates of Paradise to an ugly, dirt-covered person, suggests that it is possible to *create* a new and exemplary life in an instant, at life's last moments. But how can the work that requires a lifetime to achieve be condensed into a few brief instants?

For a better understanding, imagine the total sinner succeeding in rebuilding his old heart, cell by cell, nerve by nerve, while sitting in his bent-over position on top of the hill. Imagine that he is sitting in a time capsule, moving back through time. On his journey through time, he relives and regrets, one by one, each of the innumerable sinful acts of his life, mindful of each limb that consummated and enjoyed sinful acts and each thought of defiance of God and His laws. Invigorated by his newly reconstituted heart and mind, he erases each misdeed and reverses desires and ambitions as his past passes in review in a powerful burst of instant *teshuvah*.

The feasibility of instant *teshuvah* is confirmed by the sequel to the story in *Avodah Zarah*. The *Gemara* relates that when Rabbi Yehudah Hanasi (c. 135–c. 200 C.E.), the compiler and editor of the *Mishnah*, heard the story of the repentant sinner, he cried, "It is possible for a person to acquire his share in the World-to-Come in one hour of repentance" (*Avodah Zarah* 10b). How precious, therefore, is each moment of our lives. How rich is the potential of a man's life lasting an untold number of hours that we utilize so rarely to the fullest.

A CONCLUDING THOUGHT

The abstruse concept of instant *teshuvah* may be better understood if it is explained in terms of a process of condensation and concentration.

A space traveler moving at close to the velocity of light (186,300 miles per second) will find that the clock in his cabin slows down and virtually comes to a halt. At this speed, time and duration assume new dimensions. Processes that consume a great deal of time on earth can be accomplished in seconds of time in this spaceship traveling close to the speed of light. For example, after hurtling through space for many years, the space traveler will actually have aged only minutes or hours on *his* clock.

Nuclear reactors, atomic radiation, and biochemistry are capable of greatly accelerating biological processes. It is conceivable, therefore, that physiological and mental processes that ordinarily take a lifetime to complete, could be accomplished, *relived*, and experienced within a matter of hours.

Therefore, the experiential space and time to which our thinking has been conditioned are relative perceptions, relevant only to our specific space–time existence. Bearing this in mind, we can understand that it is conceivable that *teshuvah* transcends the limitations of space and time and that instant *teshuvah* is indeed possible. Rabbi Yehudah Hanasi said, "*Yesh koneh olamo beshaah achat*" ("It is possible to *acquire and fully possess* one's entire world in one hour").

The sages expressed it succinctly: "Great is *teshuvah*, for it reaches the *Kissei Hakavod*, the divine throne of Glory." This statement may imply that, if necessary, the *baal teshuvah* scales the vast distance from the morass of sin to the lofty heights of nearness to God within an instant.

In light of this, it becomes plausible that the recreative power of instant repentance works in two directions: first, it may retroactively transform earlier sins into relived virtues; second, it can greatly intensify even the briefest period of *teshuvah* during the final hours of a man's life.

It should be noted, however, that halachically, repentance at old age, when man is no longer challenged by an overpowering drive, is not equivalent to a fully valid *teshuvah* of a young person. On the other hand, since every deed and every thought is permanently recorded in the divine ledger, even seemingly insignificant *teshuvah* thoughts are indestructible. The prophet assures us of this when, regarding the repentant evildoer, he declares, "Let the wicked give up his ways . . . let him turn back to God, and He will have compassion on him" ("*virachameihu*") (Isaiah 55:7). God's abundant compassion magnifies each utterance of *teshuvah*, even the tormented sigh of a repentant old man, provided, of course, that it springs from deep and heartfelt remorse.

III

THE MONTH OF
TESHUVAH—TISHREI

10
ENDINGS AND BEGINNINGS

Contrary to popular opinion, God judges the world not only during the Days of Awe in the month of *Tishrei*; in fact, the entire year is the season for divine judgment. One talmudic sage holds that man is being judged every day of the year; another claims that man's deeds are assessed continually, every moment of the day (*Rosh Hashanah* 16a). The month of *Tishrei*, however, does have the distinction of being a special season of repentance and of divine judgment.

Tishrei begins with the Ten Days of *Teshuvah*, starting on Rosh Hashanah, the formal beginning of the new year, and ending with Yom Kippur, the day on which our sins are forgiven. On the fifteenth day of *Tishrei* we begin to celebrate the seven days of Sukkot, followed by the closing days of Shemini Atzeret and Simchat Torah, which, as we will see, are in their own particular way also part of the month of *teshuvah* and judgment.

The opening words of the first *Mishnah* of the tractate *Rosh Hashanah* read, "*Arbaah rashei shanim heim*" ("There are four New Year's Days in the Jewish year"[1]) the first of *Elul* is the

New Year for the tithes of animals[2]; . . . the first of *Nisan* is the
New Year for the kings and for the Pilgrimage Festivals; . . .
the first of *Tishrei* is the New Year of the calendar; . . . and on
the fifteenth of *Shevat* is the New Year of the Trees.

What the *Mishnah* is telling us is both surprising and intriguing. Ironically, the opening words of the tractate devoted to
Rosh Hashanah as the Jewish New Year imply that Rosh
Hashanah is not a New Year's Day in the universally accepted
sense, but one of four New Year's Days that occur at different
junctures throughout each calendar year. It is true that in
contemporary society we know of a variety of New Year's
days (Russian Orthodox, Moslem, Chinese), but each of these
is the beginning of the respective calendar year of a different
nation or faith. Only Judaism recognizes four dates as individual New Year's Days.

This first *Mishnah* is followed by a similar one dealing with
the subject of divine judgment: "The world is judged at four
periods in the year: . . . On Rosh Hashanah all people of the
world are judged individually, passing single file before Him
like sheep. . . . And on Sukkot, judgment is pronounced on
rainfall" (*Mishnah Rosh Hashanah* 1:2). This indicates that
Sukkot is a time when momentous decisions are made in
Heaven affecting people's livelihood during the year ahead.

ANNUAL CYCLES

Clearly, these four New Year's Days do not mark the beginnings of a year; rather they signify beginnings of concurrent
and overlapping annual cycles. Although Rosh Hashanah is
only one of the four New Year's Days, it stands out because on
this day all mankind is being judged.

Since Rosh Hashanah is a day of such pivotal importance,
why is it relegated to third place on the *Mishnah's* list of New

Year's Days? Moreover, why is Rosh Hashanah celebrated in
the seventh month? Would it not be more in keeping with its
exceptional character to celebrate it on the first day of the first
month? This apparent downgrading of the primary role of
Rosh Hashanah requires an explanation.

The Torah offers a reason for choosing the autumn month
of *Tishrei* as the time for Rosh Hashanah, rather than *Nisan*,
which occurs in the spring. *Tishrei* was selected because it
marks the end of the harvest of the past year and marks the
beginning of the season of rainfall, which nurtures the crops of
the coming year. The Torah tells us that the blessings of rain
and a bountiful harvest hinge upon our fulfillment of God's
commandments: "If you follow My laws and faithfully observe My commandments, I will grant you rains in their
season, so that the earth shall yield its produce and the trees of
the field their fruit" (Leviticus 26:3). Thus, our conduct has a
bearing on the availability of rain, and, concomitantly, the
harvests.

The life of a tree provides an instructive illustration of a
permanent record of a series of events, as each year the circum-
ference of the tree grows by another ring.

When you cut the trunk of a tree, the annual rings are
exposed in the cross section, each ring representing a year of
growth. Before your eyes is revealed the history of the tree
over its entire lifetime. A dark and narrow ring means the tree
had a poor year; a bright and wide ring indicates a year that
was abundant. Throughout the year, the ring is subject to
change, but once the ring of any given year is completed it will
not change any more; its shape and color are final. The record
of the tree's story for that year is sealed.

Just as the tree's cycle closes in *Shevat*, the agricultural cycle
comes to a close at the end of harvest time. But in *Tishrei* we
also have the beginning of the rainy season of the new year,
which will determine the growth of food in the coming year.

This explains why Rosh Hashanah is not set in the spring time, in *Nisan*, but at the "turn of the year" (*tekufat hashanah*), in the autumn, in *Tishrei*.

END AND BEGINNING
OF THE JEWISH YEAR

The entire month of *Tishrei*, and not merely the *Yom Tov* of Rosh Hashanah, represents the end of the old and the beginning of the new annual cycle. This is also evident in the Torah text, for despite the fact that Sukkot begins on the fifteenth of *Tishrei*, it is defined in the Torah as "*tekufat hashanah*" (the festival at "*the turn of the year*") (Exodus 34:22).

Thus we see that the turn of the year reaches into the second half of *Tishrei*. Rosh Hashanah is not an isolated day of remembrance; it is the overture for an entire month of *Yamim Tovim* (festivals) that bear the character of divine judgment regarding the past and of decisions made regarding the future.

JUDGMENT AND ATONEMENT

Rosh Hashanah and Yom Kippur, the *Yamim Nora'im*—the Days of Awe—are characterized by the awe a Jew feels as he is standing before *shofeit kol haaretz*, God, Who sits in judgment of the entire world but Who, at the same time, pardons and forgives.

Still, there are essential differences between Rosh Hashanah and Yom Kippur. Rosh Hashanah still has the character of a festival, day of feasting, of drinking wine and rejoicing, a *Yom Tov* when we eat a piece of apple dipped in honey and other symbolic foods as propitious omens for a sweet year, whereas Yom Kippur is marked by solemn worship. Ezra the scribe, upon arriving from Babylonia, told the people of Jerusalem on Rosh Hashanah, "Go, eat choice foods and drink sweet wines . . . do not be sad, for rejoicing in the Lord is the source of your strength" (Nehemiah 8:10). The sages of the *Talmud* questioned Ezra's failure to demand a sober and reverent demeanor, an attitude more in keeping with the serious character of the Day of Judgment. Isn't the situation of a Jew on Rosh Hashanah, they asked, comparable to that of a man awaiting a judge's verdict? The answer is that a person facing a human judge is uneasy because he fears the judge might be corrupt. But we know that our heavenly judge is the incorruptible God of forgiveness. On Rosh Hashanah we do not approach God with fear and trepidation of being judged unjustly; we stand before Him in prayer, confident that in his boundless love He will mitigate the harsh verdict we may deserve because of our poor conduct. This positive attitude is the source of the rejoicing on Rosh Hashanah that Ezra mandated. It is also the reason we do not dress in black but wear a festive white *kittel* (robe) on Rosh Hashanah.

Rosh Hashanah also differs from Yom Kippur in its liturgy. For example, although Rosh Hashanah is the Day of Judgment, we do not recite the *Viduy*, the confession of sins, as we do on Yom Kippur, when we address the God of forgiveness. On Rosh Hashanah we address Him as the Judge, asking for a comprehensive, not-guilty verdict without enumerating any specific transgressions. In our prayers on Rosh Hashanah we pray to the divine Judge to use His attribute of mercy in judging His creatures, addressing our pleas "to the One Who is merciful to His people on the day of judgment" (from the majestic hymn, "*LeEil Orech Din*").

YOM KIPPUR—THE DAY OF ATONEMENT

The Torah defines Yom Kippur as "the day on which you shall have all your sins atoned" (Leviticus 16:30). At first glance this might seem strange. If the general verdict was automatically completed on Rosh Hashanah on the basis of our past record, is there still a need for forgiveness ten days later?

Indeed there is. The Jewish people, who are fulfilling 613 commandments, are bearing a much heavier burden than the non-Jewish nations, who are required to observe only the seven categories of Noachide law. Moreover, the Jewish people are constantly exposed to the enticements of the non-Torah values of their non-Jewish environment. As a result, they have a greater need for opportunities to do *teshuvah* than the rest of the world. In light of these factors, Yom Kippur was granted to the Jewish people as a fully deserved favor to serve as a day of repentance and forgiveness. As a matter of fact, in our prayers on Yom Kippur we repeatedly express our gratitude for the special gift of this day of forgiveness. Only by dint of Yom Kippur could the innately stubborn Jewish people hope to survive as God's chosen nation and avoid complete assimilation among the nations of the world.

Whereas on Rosh Hashanah the fate of the nations of the world is being determined as to war or peace, famine or abundance, rain or drought, on Yom Kippur the status of the Jewish *individual* is finalized, his guilt or innocence, "who will live and who will die, who will enjoy tranquillity and who will suffer, who will be enriched and who will be impoverished" (from the prayer "*Unetaneh Tokef*"). The special privilege of an additional Day of Atonement gives the Jew an opportunity to make a special effort to do genuine *teshuvah* during the ten days between Rosh Hashanah and Yom Kippur. In light of this, we readily understand that since Yom Kippur addresses itself primarily to the Jewish *individual's* missteps and failings, the *Viduy*, the personal confession of sins, is an essential component of the Yom Kippur service.

VIDUY—CONFESSION OF SIN

The verbal confession of one's sins and shortcomings is a universally accepted instrument for attaining purity of soul and peace of mind. In our prayers on Yom Kippur the *Viduy* is preceded by a profession of faith wherein we state our belief in God's omniscience: "The intentional and unintentional sins You recognize; the willful and the unavoidable, the revealed and the hidden—before You they are revealed and known."

Furthermore, we clearly express our insecurity regarding the basic justification for our confession: We ask God: "*Mah nomar lefanecha*" ("What can we say before You Who dwells on high, and what can we relate before You Who dwells in the highest Heavens? Surely everything hidden and revealed, You know").

If God knows everything, why is it necessary to verbalize our confession? Moreover, we are supposed to verbalize it audibly. Why is it not enough if we think it through in the privacy of our thoughts? Don't we often communicate silently with God, in thought only? Didn't Hannah, the mother of the prophet Samuel, pray silently, as it says, "Only her lips moved, but her voice could not be heard" (1 Samuel 1:13)?

The answer to these questions appears to be a simple one. By hearing ourselves utter our remorse for past deeds and our resolve for the future, our words take on added substance and meaning. Articulating our confession makes us feel as though we were put on the stand and were testifying against ourselves.

Remorse must precede the verbalizing of certain sins committed at a certain time. The recitation of the "*Al Cheit*" then makes sense as an expression of regret followed by a resolve to give up the sin in the future. In the case of universal repentance, however, as on Yom Kippur, when we aspire individually as well as collectively to become cleansed of all our sins, it is virtually impossible to be aware of each and every one of our past missteps. It is for this reason that in the Yom Kippur confession we read, one by one, all possible categories of sins as they are enumerated in the *Viduy* of "*Al Cheit*."[3]

INTERRELATIONSHIP OF THE CATEGORIES

After expressing his regrets, a repentant should feel a sense of relief, as though a heavy burden had been lifted from his shoulders. Still, some sincere people have a problem of conscience, particularly with regard to the explicit "*Al Cheit*" confession. They wonder whether it makes any sense to confess a long list of sins, most of which they do not remember having committed, or to repeat certain categories in different wordings. They may indeed be mystified by the duplication of sins in the long "*Al Cheit*" confession. For example, the sin of *tzarut ayin* (a begrudging eye), which is listed as a separate and distinct failing, is really a subdivision of the broader category of *sinat chinam*, baseless hatred of one's fellow man, which is also mentioned in the "*Al Cheit*." More examples of such overlapping sin categories can be cited.

INTEGRATION

It is generally believed that the "*Al Cheit*" confession can be better understood if one realizes that it has a collective character. Since all Jews are responsible for one another's mistakes, we must confess even sins that we have not personally committed. Indeed, we confess in the plural, "*Al cheit shechatanu*" ("For the sin that *we* have sinned"). We do not say, "For the sin that "*I* have sinned."

Still, this assumption is not universally accepted. A confession is primarily a personal matter. Therefore, the question remains regarding those shortcomings that are unknown to us and to the entire congregation. Furthermore, how can we repent for something we are not even aware of? And if we don't repent for a sin, doesn't its omission make our confession incomplete? After all, the Torah explicitly demands that "he must personally confess the sin that he has committed" (Leviticus 5:5).

We address this problem by stating after the "*Al Cheit*" that "those [sins] that are not revealed to us are revealed and known to You, as it is said, '*Hanistarot laShem*' ('The concealed [sins] that we are unaware of are known to God')" (Deuteronomy 29:28). The truth is that since we realize many of our shortcomings will remain *nistarot* (hidden and unknown to us), we must also realize that those "*Al Cheit*" statements that we do not recognize as our own individual sins may be hidden from us but are known to God.

But God assures us in His Torah and through His prophets that He pardons all sins, especially on Yom Kippur, and also implicitly pardons those sins that are scrambled and scattered throughout the long list of the *Viduy* of "*Al Cheit*." Consequently, there is no need for each sin that appears in the comprehensive "*Al Cheit*" confession to be clearly defined. The confessing Jew actually senses that all that is expected of him is to admit that he has sinned and for the high priest to say on the people's behalf that they have transgressed. That this is the true meaning of the Torah concept of confession is made clear by the fact that the high priest confesses the sins of the people although he is ignorant of the specific sins of each individual.

The purifying function of forgiveness is described in all its detail in the Yom Kippur liturgy. It is during the *Mussaf* service that every praying Jew repeats the words enunciated by the high priest: "Before God you will be cleansed (*tit'haru*) of all your sins" (Leviticus 16:30).[4]

It is this repeated *tit'haru* that brings about the catharsis and the complete relaxation of conscience and guilt feelings so typical of the *Ne'ilah* service of Yom Kippur. Indeed, we end Yom Kippur in a jubilant mood with a spirited recital of "*Shema Yisrael*" and the sevenfold proclamation that *Hashem* (Whom *we* worship) is *Elohim*, the universal God, after which everyone is looking forward to Sukkot, the next festival of *teshuvah*, the joyous *Yom Tov* of *teshuvah mei'ahavah*, *teshuvah* out of love.

SUKKOT, THE THIRD FESTIVAL IN *TISHREI*

Sukkot, the Festival of Joy, *Zeman Simchateinu*, is the third *Yom Tov* in the month of *Tishrei*, beginning five days after Yom Kippur.

As mentioned earlier, Sukkot is defined in the Torah as *tekufat hashanah* ("year's end"). Thus, whereas Rosh Hashanah represents a first beginning of the new year, Sukkot brings the old year to a final close and ushers in the new year by proclaiming the arrival of the rainy season. The closing of the old year extends more than halfway into the month of *Tishrei*. One might view the series of *Tishrei* festivals as an ongoing process of beginning and ending, as each of the three (actually four) *Yamim Tovim* alternately faces forward and backward, beginning the new and ending the old year. The old year flows into the new year in a gradual transition rather than ending abruptly at a precise cutoff date.

KABBALAH LEHABA—RESOLVE FOR THE FUTURE

The festivals of *Tishrei* have one common denominator: *teshuvah*. Furthermore, the solemn Days of Awe are characterized by the seriousness of *teshuvah mi'yirah*, repentance out of fear of punishment, whereas Sukkot, the "Festival of Joy," is our way of expressing *teshuvah mei'ahavah*, repentance out of pure love of God and His *mitzvot*.

As mentioned earlier, genuine *teshuvah* is comprised of two elements: *charatah* (regret of past failings) and *kabbalah lehaba* (anticipation and a resolve to do better in the future). While on Yom Kippur the emphasis is on *charatah*, on Sukkot the focus is on *kabbalah lehaba*. On Yom Kippur our return to God is prompted by the realization that we have failed by misusing life's bountiful gifts. We therefore return to God along the path of asceticism, abstaining from food and drink and conjugal relations for an entire day. But having been cleansed of our sins on Yom Kippur, we are filled with happiness, which we express on Sukkot by returning to God, determined to change our way of life and from now on using God's gifts to build a life of serving Him joyfully. We are looking forward to the new year, ready to plunge into a sea of *mitzvot*.

THE *SUKKAH*

No sooner has Yom Kippur ended than we turn our attention to the *sukkah*. The *sukkah* sanctifies our entire physical and spiritual life. A chasidic saying beautifully expresses this idea: "The *sukkah* is the only *mitzvah* we fulfill with our entire body." Indeed, when sitting in the *sukkah* we are immersing ourselves—both physically and spiritually—in a *mitzvah*.

Another chasidic rabbi puts it this way: "Sitting in the *sukkah* we are wrapped in *mitzvot*: the covering above us, the walls surrounding us, and the decorations that adorn the *sukkah* form a cloak of *mitzvot* to shield us."

THE *ETROG* AND *LULAV* BUNDLE

A characteristic *mitzvah* of Sukkot, one that fascinates young and old, Jew and non-Jew alike, is the *lulav* set consisting of four kinds of plants. The *aravah* (willow twigs) produces neither edible fruit nor fragrance. It represents raw material: its wood is used in the construction of houses, furniture, and ships, and it provides fuel for heating and cooking. The *hadassim* (myrtle twigs) give off a pleasing fragrance. The beautiful *lulav* is a branch of the fruit-bearing date palm. And the *etrog* (the citron) is a fruit that excels in its fragrance, taste, and beauty. The *lulav* set thus comprises all the necessities of life and sources of physical enjoyment: raw materials, nutrition, fragrance, and beauty, the highest form of human enjoyment.[5] In making circuits around the *bimah* with the *lulav* set, we dedicate all necessities and pleasures of life to God. To summarize: By enveloping ourselves in the *mitzvah* of *sukkah* and dedicating our needs and sources of pleasure to God during each day of Sukkot, we are making an auspicious start for our conduct in the new year.

It is characteristic of the inner symmetry of Jewish traditions that Sukkot, like Rosh Hashanah, has a universal character in that it involves the well-being of all the nations of the world. The Talmud tells us that the seventy bulls that were offered as burnt-offerings on the altar during Sukkot were to protect all the seventy nations of the world from suffering, to seek atonement for them, and to seek peace for all peoples (*Bamidbar Rabbah* 21).[6]

Rashi, who witnessed the murder of entire Jewish communities by the "holy" Crusaders in the Rhineland, made a poignant comment: "As long as Israel was sacrificing the seventy bulls, the nations of the world were nourished with additional life power. After the destruction of the Temple in Jerusalem it became impossible for Jews to bring these offerings. Many nations grew progressively weaker until they were *kalim mei'eileihem*—they faded into oblivion and disappeared from the stage of history."

This interpretation of the seventy sacrifices is not merely a noble display by the talmudic sages of empathy with a suffering world; it is based on biblical prophecy. Zechariah, one of the last prophets, foretells that the nations of the world "will ascend every year to prostrate themselves before the

King, God, Master of Legions, to celebrate the festival of Sukkot (Zechariah 14:16). The prophecy implies that the nations of the world will prosper and will come to the Temple to thank God for their material well-being, which makes Sukkot, like Rosh Hashanah, a festival of universal significance involving all nations of the world.[7]

HOSHANA RABBAH, THE LAST DAY OF SUKKOT

On Sukkot our attention is directed to the harvest of the outgoing year. The *lulav* set, especially the willow twigs, which grow on the banks of a stream, remind us of our dependence on water. It is this dependence on rainfall that lends a serious undertone to the Festival of Joy and particularly so to Hoshana Rabbah, the last day, which, according to Torah law, we are obligated to spend in the *sukkah*. The solemn character of Hoshana Rabbah finds expression in the traditional services of that day. Whereas on the preceding days of Sukkot we made one circuit around the *bimah* with the *lulav*, on Hoshana Rabbah we make seven circuits, as if summing up the meaning of the *lulav* of the six preceding days in the perspective of the seventh day.[8]

In the Jewish tradition, Hoshana Rabbah is considered the day that God applies the final seal to His judgment of the rainfall in the coming year. Therefore, notwithstanding the prevailing general aura of happiness of Sukkot, Hoshana Rabbah introduces a number of features of the services of the High Holy Days and has a semblance of a *Yom Hadin*, Judgment Day.

SHEMINI ATZERET, THE FESTIVAL OF THE RAINS

Ironically, the rains, which are eagerly anticipated, are most unwelcome on Sukkot itself since the *mitzvah* of dwelling in the *sukkah* can be fulfilled only in the absence of rain. Actually, Sukkot gives you the feeling of bidding farewell to the carefree days of summer outdoor living and prepares you to return to your sheltered home where you are protected from the coming heavy rains.

Therefore, *Tefillat Geshem*, the solemn prayer for rain, is recited only on Shemini Atzeret, the closing festival, after the scriptural commandment of *sukkah*-dwelling is over. Its hauntingly beautiful traditional melody is chanted by the *chazzan* (cantor), who is dressed in the white *kittel* (robe), evoking the mood of the Days of Awe.

According to *Halachah*, if it rains so hard on Sukkot that the rain would spoil the food, we are exempt from the obligation of eating in the *sukkah*. Rain on Sukkot is considered a sign of rejection that should make us feel humbled, like a servant who pours a cup of wine for his master, and the master spills a jug of water in his face (*Sukkah* 29a).

The sages state that only an insensitive person (a *hedyot*) would stay in the *sukkah* during a drenching rain. This seems like an uncharacteristically harsh condemnation of the person who in his piety is ready to suffer the inconvenience of a heavy rain in an effort to fulfill the *mitzvah* of *sukkah*.

Perhaps the sages want to accentuate the fact that the *mitzvah* of *sukkah* and rainfall are mutually exclusive. While the *sukkah* represents a farewell to the dry season, one still looks forward to the arrival of the blessed rains shortly after Sukkot. However, if the rains come prematurely—before Sukkot has ended—then it would be contrary to the intent of Sukkot for us to stay in the *sukkah*. A person staying in the *sukkah* in spite of the rain is displaying insensitivity and a lack of understanding of the *mitzvah* of *sukkah*. By commanding us to live in the *sukkah* so close to the onset of the rainy season, God makes each day without rain a favorable sign of His grace. Rainfall during Sukkot means that this sign of grace has been withheld. We show true understanding of this by leaving the *sukkah*, albeit reluctantly, when it rains.

THE FOURTH AND FINAL
TISHREI FESTIVAL

The symmetry that prevails in all our *Yamim Tovim* is clearly evident in the festival of Shemini Atzeret/Simchat Torah, the two days following Sukkot proper. Just as Pesach and Shavuot are closely linked, so too are Sukkot and Shemini Atzeret. Shavuot commemorates the giving of the Torah, and Shemini Atzeret/Simchat Torah are dedicated to the true spiritual joy of the Torah. Analogous to Shavuot, Shemini Atzeret has no tangible symbols (no *sukkah* and no *lulav* set).[9]

In keeping with the theme of the month of *Tishrei*, that is, ending the old and beginning anew, on Simchat Torah the last chapter in Deuteronomy is read, followed by the reading of the first chapters of the Torah in Genesis. The combined reading of these two sections is preceded by ecstatic singing and dancing as the Torah scrolls are carried around the *bimah* in seven rousing circuits. The thinking Jew sees in this joyous but controlled dancing a manifestation of *iruv* and *verur*, confusion and clarification. The semblance of the excessive corporeal joy of dancing, eating, and drinking seems to stand in sharp contrast with the experience of spiritual delight. The character of the festivities is also apparent in the utter caution with which the dancing is proceeding, the care that is taken not to drop the Torah scroll and not to push or hurt a fellow dancer. It is a demonstration of the idea that man is responsible for upholding the spirituality and sanctity of life under all of life's conditions.

TESHUVAH MEI'AHAVAH—REPENTANCE
OUT OF LOVE

The seven joyous circuits of Simchat Torah (evening and morning) with the Torah scrolls in hand are parallel to the seven solemn circuits of Hoshana Rabbah, carrying the *lulav*.

The seven Simchat Torah circuits symbolize our spiritual rejoicing in the gift of the Torah, as the seven Hoshana Rabbah circuits represent the dedication of all our material wants and needs to God's altar.

In a remarkable demonstration of *teshuvah mei'ahavah*, we translate the joyous *Yom Tov* of Sukkot and its attendant *mitzvot* into a resolve to improve our way of life, not by ascetic withdrawal and fasting but by enjoying the delights of life and using them in the service of the Torah.

CONCLUSION

Sukkot and Simchat Torah, the festivals of the second half of the New Year's month, arouse the fascination of Jews and non-Jews alike. People's curiosity is piqued by the strange sight of Jews building outdoor booths covered with branches, Jews proudly walking in the streets carrying palm branches and precious silver or wooden boxes containing a citrus fruit. Ironically, this extended and demonstrative festival had not been taken seriously by many uncommitted Jews. Except for the *hakafot* on the night of Simchat Torah, they had paid scant attention to the festival, which they apparently perceived as an anticlimax coming after the emotionally charged Days of Awe.

In recent decades, however, a change has taken place. The estranged Jews, too, have begun to realize that the mood of the High Holy Days reaches its culmination in Sukkot. They have apparently learned to understand that by taking the Sukkot season lightly one foregoes the *teshuvah mei'ahavah*, return to God for love, that is inherent in this festival of unbounded joy and happiness. In closing, we pray that the nations of the world will understand that the prophets and the talmudic sages viewed the Sukkot holiday as the universal festival for the benefit of all the nations that comprise humankind.

EPILOGUE

In Remembrance

This book, which explores the relations of man to his Creator, is dedicated to the memory of Rafael Nussbaum and his two sons, Morty and Shabsai, who perished in the Holocaust.

In 1941, the family left Holland for Antwerp on their way to Switzerland. Since most of the Jews of Antwerp were engaged in the production of diamonds and furs—commodities that were essential to the German war effort in Russia—the Jews of that city were not deported at first and were permitted to move about unmolested. One day, alighting from a street car and waiting for an agent who would take them to safety in Switzerland, Rafael and his wife were accosted by a Nazi who brutally grabbed Rafael and abducted him while his wife watched helplessly. He was never heard from again.

Rafael's son Morty, a valiant young man, always eager to help others, was in Marseilles, France, waiting for reliable guides to escort the family across the French Alps into Switzerland. Embarking on a mission of mercy, he entered a local hotel where many refugees were waiting for an opportunity to escape to Switzerland. Just then the Germans conducted a raid, rounding up Jews for transport to a concentration camp. Silently and with bowed heads, the unfortunate Jews climbed into the waiting trucks. Knowing that under the Vichy regime his Dutch passport would shield him from deportation, Morty felt safe. However, when the German brusquely demanded to see his identification, he discovered to his dismay that in his hurry to answer the telephone call of one of the refugees, he had left his passport in his room. His protestations were to no avail.

His older brother Samuel, at some risk to himself, attempted to take the passport to Morty in the camp, only to be turned back by the guards at the gate, who did not even bother to look at the document. Samuel considered himself fortunate not to be arrested. Shortly thereafter Morty was sent to a concentration camp along with the others.

After the war, a friend of Morty's who survived and returned to The Hague reported that in 1944 he had been together with Morty in a concentration camp near Warsaw. He related that Morty had volunteered for a work detail because some of his close friends, to whom he had been giving moral and practical support, had been inducted into the slave labor gang. Morty's mother, who survived the war in Switzerland and had returned to Holland, was overjoyed to receive a sign of life about her long lost son; her hope for his safe return rekindled. But it was not to be. Like his father, he was never heard from again.

Morty's younger brother by two years, Shabsai, was a gentle, loving soul in a frail body. A studious boy, he immersed himself in the Talmud day and night, allowing himself no more than four or five hours of sleep. Troubled by his pale and emaciated looks, his mother insisted that he needed more rest. When he did wake up an hour or two later than usual, he silently bemoaned the loss of precious hours of learning. Seeing his inner torment, his mother allowed him to go back to his routine despite his pallor and fatigue. His fellow students at the *yeshivah* of Heide (north of Antwerp) knew him as the kindest and most idealistic of their group, a young man always ready to help other students with their studies.

Shortly after the German invasion of Belgium, despite the heroic efforts of its illustrious head rabbi, Feivel Shapiro, the *yeshivah* was forced to close. Shabsai, along with a friend, went into hiding in Holland in a place his sister (whose husband had recently died in the Mauthausen concentration camp) had found for them. In their hideout, the two boys continued their Torah studies, day and night. When his family left Holland in an attempt to flee to Switzerland via France, Shabsai refused to leave his hiding place to join them. Although his hiding place offered no real safety, traveling through Belgium and France was fraught with danger, too. Many people had been caught crossing the Alps into Switzerland, only to be stopped by Swiss border guards and handed back to the Germans. Since neither staying nor leaving was really safe, he preferred continuing his studies in his secret hideaway. Soon thereafter, the Dutch underground warned his sister that his hiding place was not safe any more, and he was forced to move to a different location near his sister in Amsterdam. One day, the Germans barged into his hiding place, arresting all occupants. Shabsai was never heard from again.

Rafael Nussbaum, father of ten children and a *baal tefillah* (cantor) with a lyrical voice, was a well-to-do merchant who owned a small bank and a prosperous wholesale business in Rzeszow (Reisha), Poland. Both his partners were respected members of the community. To Rafael's deep dismay, one day in 1929, during the Depression, one of the partners absconded, taking with him a substantial amount of money he had withdrawn from the business. A few months later, the other partner made off with an even larger amount.

Rafael, gravely disappointed and despondent, left home, deeply ashamed at defaulting on creditors who had trusted him. He moved to Holland, where he started a small business and was able to begin paying off his creditors. Living alone in a small apartment, he wrote his wife that as soon as he settled his debts he would send for his family.

Late one afternoon, a tall, disheveled stranger with a slightly bent back entered Rafael's office. Rafael was visibly shaken, and his face turned ashen. He stared at the stranger without uttering a word. Suddenly, he broke the silence and greeted the guest with a subdued "*Shalom aleichem!*" The guest stood there, shamefacedly avoiding Rafael's eyes. The man who had entered the office was the second partner who had ruined Rafael's reputation and business.

The man said that hunger had driven him to overcome his shame and beg for alms. He explained that he had spent all his money, no, *their* money, on his daughter's wedding. Rafael, unable to bear the sight of his former partner's humiliation, told him to wait. He spent the entire evening collecting donations for "someone who lost his business and has to resort to picking up cigarette butts in one of Antwerp's synagogues to still his hunger."

Late at night he returned and handed his guest a substantial sum of money, the proceeds of his collection, suggesting that he return to Antwerp and open a small store. Deeply moved by the noble spirit of the man whose life he had destroyed, the guest began to cry. With a tear-choked voice he whispered, "Forgive me," and then he turned and headed for the station to catch the train to Antwerp.

That same night Rafael wrote his wife that she should join him without delay.

Rafael Nussbaum and his sons Morty and Shabsai exemplify the majestic refinement of a life devoted to Torah values. They gave their lives *al kiddush Hashem* (for the sanctification of God's name) along with six million *kedoshim*. Their souls ascended to Heaven, but no tombstone marks their grave. Their rectitude and boundless faith are their everlasting memorials. May this book, sponsored by close relatives, serve to perpetuate their remembrance.

APPENDIX

Additional Sources

AGGADIC AND MYSTICAL SOURCES

Insights of the Sages Regarding *Teshuvah*

A person must verbalize his failings . . . for the judgment of one who verbalizes his sins will be determined by the King, the Holy One Blessed is He, Himself (*Zohar*, *Bamidbar*). [A person may be prompted to return to God because of suffering and adversities. However, if the sinner turns to God in a self-willed confession, the response will come from the addressee, the Creator Himself.]

When a person does *teshuvah*, even the evil impulse testifies in his favor (*Zohar Chadash*, Ruth 124).

When a wicked Jew does *teshuvah* he is accepted by the *Shechinah* as a *tzaddik* (righteous man) and is judged as though he had never sinned.

Said the Holy One Blessed is He to Israel: "Children, as long as the Gates of Prayer are still open, please do *teshuvah*, for in this world I can be bribed. But when I sit in judgment in the World-to-Come, I do not take bribes." [In his life on earth, man can still change, and his Creator helps him to do *teshuvah*. This means that God is prepared not to punish man, offering him another chance. Such latitude is not available any more once the sinner has departed this world.]

The Messengers of *Teshuvah*

The *Gemara* (*Chagigah* 12b) relates that there exists one angel whose feet are standing on earth while his head reaches the *chayot*, the angels that surround the divine throne (*Kissei Hakavod*) of world management, where all *teshuvah* is registered.

This aggadic allegory conveys the idea of the close association that connects the earthly and heavenly realms. The interaction between Heaven and earth is carried out by the angels, who are described as *ratzoh vashov* (dashing to and fro) (Ezekiel 1:14), running forward to fulfill their assignments and returning after completing them. Viewed from the perspective of *teshuvah*, this means that the angels carry "upward" all messages of *teshuvah* and then return to earth, bringing with them forgiveness.

All the Way to the *Kissei Hakavod*

"The power of *teshuvah* is great, for as soon as a person contemplates doing *teshuvah* he immediately ascends—not just ten miles, not even twenty miles . . . but a journey of five hundred years . . . to the highest heaven, until he stands in front of the *Kissei Hakavod*, the heavenly throne" (*Pesikta Rabbati* 44).

Teshuvah—A Remedy

"There is a remedy for every affliction in the world, and the remedy for the *yetzer hara* (the evil tendency) is *teshuvah*" (*Midrash Tanchumah* 58:1).

The sages said that sin results from mental aberration. "No man sins unless a spirit of madness enters into him" (*Sotah* 3a). But even for such mental deviations God provides a cure—*teshuvah*.

He Refused to Do Teshuvah

" 'A man's pride will humiliate him' (Proverbs 29:23). This verse refers to Adam. The Holy One Blessed is He wanted Adam to do *teshuvah*, but Adam declined. Said the Holy One Blessed is He to Adam, 'Even now, you can still do *teshuvah*, and I will receive you [with forgiveness].' Said Adam, 'I refuse.'

"Since he pridefully resisted doing *teshuvah*, God lowered him down and drove him out of the Garden of Eden" (*Numbers Rabbah* 2:5).

How remote is this aggadic exposition from the concept of original sin. If Adam would have agreed to change his attitude and set aside his wish to be like God, he would have been permitted to stay in the ideal world of Eden (*Bikkurim* 2a).

Inner Shame

"May it be Your will that You instill in our hearts the desire to do a perfect *teshuvah*, so that we will not be ashamed in front of our fathers in the World-to-Come" (*Berachot* 4b).

This aggadic statement opens up a broader meaning of *teshuvah*. Here *teshuvah* is not prompted by the sinner's personal need but is motivated by a broader need not to break with the faith and traditions in which he was raised and not to snap the thread of continuity. He feels disappointment and shame over his conduct because he is destroying the continued growth of the ideals his fathers fought and died for and because he is betraying his heritage.

The *Yetzer Hara* of the Future

"*Teshuvah* is an ongoing process, and even the righteous are in a permanent state of *teshuvah*. Of course, they do not repent of outright sins, but they are remorseful over the fact that they did not yet achieve the highest degree of spiritual perfection attainable and did not use to the fullest all the opportunities available to them. They repent of minutes that were wasted, of not exerting all efforts at advancing the cause of Torah" (The Sefat *Emet*, Rabbi Yehudah Aryeh Leib Alter, the Gerer *rebbe*, 1847–1905).

The Heavenly Gate of *Teshuvah*

Toward the close of Yom Kippur, in the *Ne'ilah* service, we address God with a request that seems to be paradoxical. We ask, "Open the [heavenly] gate for us at this time when the gate closes."

How are we to understand this incongruity?

We imply with this fervent plea that the gate does not close irrevocably, that darkness does not descend unconditionally. There are exceptions even to the most rigorous rules. Yes, even the decree stating "Since the destruction of the *Bet Hamikdash*, the gates of prayer were closed" is subject to exemptions, for these gates will swing wide open for tear-soaked prayers and for genuine *teshuvah*.

Such "openings" and cracks are evident throughout the entire spectrum of the God–man relationship. God's word is not "the last word." And so we pray on Yom Kippur that the gates of forgiveness be reopened.

The story of man in the Garden of Eden is a prime example of the modification of one of God's unalterable decrees. When Adam's wife sinned, she brought about irreversible death for man. Yet, at the very moment that God mandated death, stating, "For dust you are, and to dust you shall return," Adam "named his wife Eve, 'the mother of all *life*' " (Genesis 4:19–20). How could Adam justify giving her this name, which seemed to challenge God's decree of death? Adam saw an "opening," a way out for her. Instead of "wifehood," which was subject to mortality, he assigned to her the primary role of motherhood, which, in a way, made her immortal.

Abraham, Champion for Righteousness

Jeremiah asked the age-old question, "Why does the way of the wicked prosper?" (Jeremiah 12:1).

Indeed, the wicked usually are successful because single-mindedly they pursue their evil goals. In the confusing world of *iruv*, of mix-up of good and evil, they often dedicate themselves with tenacity to the rape of justice. The righteous, on the other hand, resign themselves to the apparent success of crime and violence. They do not fight with the courage of their convictions and therefore often do not attain the power and influence they deserve. If the righteous would fight for justice as valiantly and with the same determination as the evildoers pursue their nefarious ambitions, they would triumph decisively.

Abraham's life proves that failure and defeat need not be the inevitable lot of the righteous. Standing alone against a pagan world, he undauntedly championed the cause of justice and righteousness in the name of *Hashem*. He became the *Av Hamon Goyim* ("the father of a multitude of nations") (Genesis 17:5), and these nations are blessed because of him. Furthermore, Abraham received the total reward that would have gone to the ten generations that preceded him had they not been sinful (*Avot* 5:3). Historically, Abraham was mankind's universal heir.

Teshuvah Greater than Charity

Why is *teshuvah* greater than charity? Because charity you may happen to give to someone who does not deserve it, voiding your act of philanthropy. But when you do *teshuvah* you give *mei'atzmo*, of yourself. You actually give your "self."

The World Created with *Teshuvah*

"The Holy One Blessed is He wanted to create the world, but it could not endure until He created *teshuvah*" (*Zohar*, Genesis 90).

Since *bechirah* (freedom of choice) was made an intrinsic part of man's personality, his existence would not be possible without *teshuvah*, which offers man the opportunity to repent and be forgiven.

The Gentile Nations

"The Holy One Blessed is He is looking forward to the time when the nations of the world will do *teshuvah*, so that He will be able to take them under His wings" (*Numbers Rabbah* 13).

After the prophet Jonah admonished the people of Nineveh, they changed their ways, but only temporarily. They soon slid back to their former wickedness. But if the Gentile nations would sincerely and permanently do *teshuvah*—politically as well as socially—then they could permanently enter the realm of God.

Pharaoh Refused to Do *Teshuvah*

"God showed Pharaoh the way to do *teshuvah*. For God did not want to bring the plagues upon him without warning him to do *teshuvah*" (*Exodus Rabbah* 12:1).

This sounds unbelievable, but the truth is that if Pharaoh would have granted freedom to the Jews and would have ceased to oppress them, he could have been saved. This means that Moses' repeated pleas to Pharaoh to let the people go were not a deceptive ploy but a genuine offer to save him and his people from impending disaster.

HALACHIC SOURCES

Rambam (Maimonides), *Yad Hachazakah*

Hilchot Teshuvah, Chapter 1

Halachah 1. If a person transgresses any of the *mitzvot* of the Torah, whether a positive command or a negative command, whether he does so willingly or inadvertently, when he repents and returns from his sin he must confess before God, blessed is He, as it is stated, "If a man or a woman commit any of the sins of man . . . they must confess the sin that they committed" (Numbers 5:6–7).

This refers to a verbal confession. This confession is a positive command.

The Confession

How does one confess? He says: "I implore You, God, I sinned, I transgressed, I committed iniquity before You by doing the following. . . . Behold, I regret and I am embarrassed by my deeds. I promise never to repeat this act again."

These are the essential elements of the confessional prayer. Whoever confesses profusely and elaborates on these matters is worthy of praise.

Those who bring sin-offerings or guilt-offerings must also [confess their sins] when they bring their sacrifices for their inadvertent or willful transgressions. Their sacrifices will not atone for their sins until they also repent and make a verbal confession, as it is written, "He shall confess upon it the sin he has committed" (Leviticus 5:5).

Convicted Sinners

Similarly, those obligated to be executed or flogged by the court do not attain atonement through their punishments unless they also repent and confess. Similarly, someone who injures his fellow or damages his property does not attain atonement, even though he pays him what he owes, until he confesses and makes a commitment never to do such a thing again.

Hilchot Teshuvah, Chapter 2

Halachah 1. [Who has attained] complete *teshuvah*? A person who confronts the same situation in which he sinned and has the potential to commit [the sin again], yet abstains and does not commit it because of his *teshuvah* alone and not because of fear or a lack of strength.

For example, a person engaged in illicit sexual relations with a woman meets with her in privacy, in the same country. Although his love for her and his physical power still persist, he nevertheless abstains and does not transgress. This is a complete *baal teshuvah*. This was implied by King Solomon when he said, "Remember your Creator in the days of your youth [before the bad days come and the years draw near when you will say: 'I have no desire for them']" (Ecclesiastes 12:1).

Instant Teshuvah

If the sinner does not repent until his old age, at a time when he is incapable of doing what he did before, even though this is not a high level of repentance, he is still a *baal teshuvah*.

Even if he transgressed throughout his entire life and repented on the day of his death, all his sins are forgiven, as it is stated, "Before the sun, the light, the moon, or the stars are darkened and the clouds return after the rain." (Ecclesiastes 12:2)—this refers to the day of death. Thus we can infer that if one remembers his Creator before he dies, he is forgiven.

Although repentance at an advanced age is not considered the ideal form of *teshuvah*, it is, nevertheless, effective.

Repentance

Halachah 2. What constitutes *teshuvah*? A sinner should abandon his sins and remove them from his thoughts, resolving in his heart never to commit them again, as it says, "Let the wicked abandon his ways" (Isaiah 55:7). Similarly, he must regret the past, as it is stated, "After I returned, I regretted" (Jeremiah 31:18).

[One must reach the level where] the *Yode'a ta'alumot* (He Who knows the hidden) will testify concerning him that he will never return to his sin again, as it is written, "We will no longer say to the work of our hands, 'You are our gods' " (Hosea 14:4).

Halachah 3. Anyone who verbalizes his confession without resolving in his heart to abandon [sin] can be compared to [a person] who immerses himself [in a *mikvah*] while [holding a dead] lizard in his hand. His immersion will be of no avail until he casts away the lizard.

Sins Against One's Fellow Man

Halachah 5. It is very commendable for a penitent to make a public confession and announce his failings and reveal to others the sins he committed against his fellow, telling them, "I have sinned against so-and-so, and this-and-this is what I did to him, and today I repent and I regret what I did." If in his pride he fails to publicize his failings but covers them up, his *teshuvah* is not complete, as it says, "He who covers up his faults will not succeed" (Proverbs 28:13). To what does this refer? To sins a person committed against his fellow man. But sins a person committed against God he need not publicize himself; it would be considered impudence if he did.

Hilchot Teshuvah, **Chapter 3**

Yom Hadin

Halachah 3. Just as a person's merits are weighed at the time of his death, so, too, are the sins of every inhabitant of the world weighed together with his merits every year on the festival of Rosh Hashanah. If he is found to be a righteous man [his verdict] is sealed for life.

Hilchot Teshuvah, **Chapter 7**

Repenting Middot *(Character Traits)*

Halachah 3. A person should not think that repentance is only necessary for those sins that involve deeds such as lewdness, robbery, or theft. Rather, just as a person is obligated to repent these, so too must he search out the evil character traits he has. He must repent anger, hatred, envy, frivolity, the pursuit of money and honor, the pursuit of gluttony, and the like. He must repent all [of the above].

These sins are more serious than those that involve a deed. If a person is attached to these it is more difficult to separate himself. In this context it is written, "Let the wicked abandon his path and the crooked man, his designs" (Isaiah 55:7).

Halachah 4. A *baal teshuvah* should not consider himself distant from the level of the righteous because of the sins and transgressions he committed. This is not true. He is beloved and desirable before the Creator as if he had never sinned.

Halachah 6. Teshuvah is great for it draws a person close to the *Shechinah*, as it is written, "Return, O Israel to God, your Lord" (Hosea 14:2), and it is written, " 'If you will return, O Israel,' declares God, 'You will return to Me' " (Jeremiah 4:1). Implied is that there exists only one address you can turn to—God!

Teshuvah brings near those who were far removed. Previously, this person was hated by God, detested, far removed, and an abomination. Now he is beloved and desirable, close and beloved.

GLOSSARY

Aggadah—Nonlegal portion of the Talmud.

Avon—Purposeful sin.

Baal teshuvah—Returnee to Torah observance.

Berur—Clarification.

Beshogeig—Inadvertently.

Bet Hamikdash—Holy Temple in Jerusalem.

Chalutz—Pioneer coming to *Eretz Yisrael*.

Chasidut—Chasidic movement of spiritual revival.

Cheit Adam Harishon—Adam's sin.

Deveikut—Attachment to God.

Go'el hadam—Blood avenger.

Halachah—Legal part of Jewish traditional literature.

Hashem—God.

Hashgachah Kelalit—God's supervision of the totality of Nature.

Hashgachah Peratit—Divine Providence for each individual.

Hastarat Panim—Hiding of Divine guidance.

Iruv—Mix-up of good and evil; confusion.

Kabbalah—Jewish mysticism.

Kedushah—Sanctity.

Kiddush—Sanctification, ceremonial blessing over wine, recited on *Shabbat* and Festivals.

Kissei Hakavod—Divine throne.

Lashon hara—Gossip, slander, talebearing.

Mashal—Parable.

Mashiach—Messiah, the Redeemer who will rebuild the Temple and usher in the Messianic Age.

Mitzvah—Commandment.

Mussar—Ethics. Movement of ethical revival through self-examination.

Neshamah—The soul.

P'shat—Plain meaning of biblical texts.

Rebbe—Chasidic rabbi.

Ribbono shel Olam—Master of the Universe.

Rosh yeshivah—Dean of a talmudical college.

Sefer Hazichronot—Book of Remembrances.

Sefirot—Spheres or vessels through which the Light of the Creator emanates.

Shechinah—Divine presence.

Shegogot—Unintentional sinful acts.

Shogeig—Unwitting transgressor.

Sod—Secret, kabbalistic wisdom.

Tefillin—Phylacteries.

Tehillim—Book of Psalms.

Teshuvah—Repentance.

Teshuvah mei'ahavah—Repentance out of love.

Teshuvah miyirah—Repentance out of fear.

Tikkun—Final restoration.

Tziruf—Combination.

Viduy—Confessional prayer.

Yeshivah—Talmudical college.

Yetzer hara—Evil inclination.

Yetzer hatov—Good inclination.

Zechuyot—Merits.

Zedonot—Purposeful transgressions.

NOTES

INTRODUCTION

1. A wide-ranging study of the lives of Adam, Cain, and David is presented in the author's previous book, *Semblance and Reality* (New York: Ktav, 1991). The present work focuses exclusively on the aspects of repentance and forgiveness in their lives, developing novel insights on this subject, especially in the case of King David's form of *teshuvah*.

The biblical-historical review of the lives of the great men of *teshuvah* is followed by the story of contemporary *teshuvah* as exemplified by the return to his people and his God by the impressive figure of Nathan Birnbaum and the *teshuvah* of his family.

CHAPTER 1

1. One wonders if it is coincidental that the serpent's curse, "Dust you shall eat, all the days of your life" (Genesis 3:14), also revolves around dust? Might there be a connection between the curse that dust would become the serpent's food and man being characterized

as dust (*"affar atta"*—"You are dust")? The serpent had stressed man's God-like quality as opposed to his *"affar,"* earthlike side. The serpent, the personification of the seduction of man, will from now on be identified as a creature immersed in dust.

CHAPTER 2

1. *Hastarat Panim*, the hiding of divine guidance and the elimination of access to one's Creator, is the root of human suffering.

2. Ibn Ezra says: "Some say the sign was a horn (*Bereishit Rabbah* 22); others say that God gave him courage and removed his fear; I [Ibn Ezra] think that God performed a sign for him so that he believed himself to be invulnerable, and Scripture does not reveal the nature of the sign." Malbim, quoting others, says that the sign was that God gave him leprosy so that any potential murderer was afraid to come near him. (Finkel).

3. It should be noted that Cain did not really accept his punishment, since he argued with God regarding its severity and the concomitant danger of being killed.

4. David displayed a forgiving attitude toward his enemies: Saul, Shimi ben Gera, Naval, Absalom, and by not sparing the lives of the killers of his opponent Ish-Boshet, the son of Saul.

5. The *Midrash* (*Bereishit Rabbah* 13) comments that by saying *"va'ocheil"* ("I did eat [from the forbidden fruit]") (Genesis 3:12), Adam implied *"va'ocheil od"* ("In the future, too, I will eat [from the forbidden fruit]").

CHAPTER 3

1. The Jews were given three *mitzvot* to fulfill after the conquest of the Promised Land: to choose a king; to wipe out the descendants of Amalek; and to build the Temple, as stated in the Torah—"Seek out His presence and go there" (Deuteronomy 12:5; also Rambam, *Hilchot Melachim* 1:1, based on *Sanhedrin* 20b).

2. We must remember that Joshua did not conquer the entire

country. It fell to David to complete this task. When the Philistines moved into the valleys of Israel in the wake of the defeat and death of Saul, fighting a war to secure peace and independence became David's first priority.

3. In accordance with Deuteronomy 20:10–12, "When you approach a city to wage war against it, you must propose a peaceful settlement. If the city responds peacefully and opens its gates to you, all the people inside shall become your subjects and serve you. If they reject your peace offer and declare war, you shall lay siege to the city. . . ." [Finkel]

4. It may not be fully realized that Saul, the first Jewish king, passed through two opposing phases in his monarchy. Initially he was the proverbial "*nechba el hakeilim*" ("the meek one, hiding among the baggage") (1 Samuel 10:22), which was in tune with the Torah's royal charter. But when Samuel told him after the war against Amalek that he was too humble for the role of king, Saul adopted the stance of an authoritative "*rosh shivtei Yisrael*" ("head of the tribes of Israel") (1 Samuel 15:17), becoming a ferocious fighter for the preservation of his royal lineage in line with Samuel's charter. Saul's ambivalence foreshadowed the concessions David would eventually make by adopting the contemporary dictatorial royal charter.

5. 1 Samuel 21:8; see Rashi.

6. The priest, in fact, did join David's opposition when he teamed up with Adoniyahu in his attempt to seize David's throne before Solomon could inherit the monarchy.

7. The Torah's charter delineates the ethical code for an Israelite king: He must not accumulate many horses. He also must not have many wives. He should not accumulate very much silver and gold, and he must write a copy of the Torah and be in awe of God.

Samuel's charter stresses the absolute rights of royalty: The king has the right to recruit young men as his charioteers and horsemen; they will have to plow his fields and reap his harvest. He will draft young women as cooks and bakers. He has the right to impose taxes, to requisition male and female slaves, and put them to work (1 Samuel 8:11–18). [Finkel]

8. *Halachah* permits a soldier to marry a *yefat to'ar*, a beautiful non-Jewish woman taken captive in war. The Torah permits this relationship only as a concession to man's natural desires, which are

heightened in the life of a soldier, who is away from home for a long
time. Yet, the Torah places limitations on the soldier in order to
discourage such marriages. He must wait three months before being
intimate with her (*Yevamot* 48b). She must shave her head and let her
fingernails grow to make her less attractive. And she must mourn her
parents for thirty days. She is given twelve months to make up her
mind to convert (Deuteronomy 21:10–14; Rambam, *Melachim* 8:6).
In a prolonged war, where the soldiers are away from home for an
extended period, they would succumb to the temptations of the
"captive women" and be influenced by their pagan ways of life.
Rashi, quoting Tanchumah, explains, "Scripture is making this concession only in view of man's carnal desires. For if God would not
permit him to take her as a wife, he would still marry her, although
she would then be forbidden to him. However, if he does marry her,
in the end he will hate her." This would lead to a weakening of the
moral fiber of the entire nation.

9. David, the great warrior, was a soft father who sometimes
made questionable decisions. Was this a reaction to Saul's authoritarian treatment of his daughters and son, Jonathan? At any rate,
David's permissive attitude had tragic repercussions in his monarchy
and family life.

Must we assume that it was impossible for David to try a new
kind of warfare in the midst of cruel barbarism, a strategy based on
reason and being satisfied with minimal accomplishments? The sages
of the Talmud tell us that Joshua, at the start of his war of conquest,
did try a policy of flexibility, offering the Canaanites the option of
leaving the country or accepting the Noachide laws rather than being
totally destroyed. But unlike David, Joshua was in full control of his
officers and men. Besides, Joshua was not beset with critics, dissent-
ers, and corrupt and treacherous politicians.

10. This was true especially in the period of the wars against
Edom and Moab. It may have been Jo'ab's harsh methods of that
period that Nathan the prophet was alluding to when he said, "You
have shed too much blood."

11. It was for this reason that toward the end of David's reign,
Jo'ab acted against the king's wishes by publicly supporting Adoni-
yahu in a coup that would have placed him on the throne instead of
David's younger son Solomon, whom Jo'ab considered too young,

too intellectual, and too idealistic to win the battle against the practical militarists and politicians whom even David could not fully control.

12. Realizing the grave risks, David prepared the political ground for Solomon, the king of peace, by charging him with the completion of David's unfinished tasks: the elimination of the last remnant of the old-guard warriors and politicians: Jo'ab, who was a great military commander, but unwilling to learn and change, and Shimi ben Gera, a man so devoted to Saul that he could never reconcile himself to the termination of Saul's dynasty. The removal of these men, which seemingly constituted a single act of bloodshed in the life of King Solomon brought upon themselves by their careless behavior, would make possible the purification of the nation's political conscience.

CHAPTER 4

1. Later in life David devoted himself to judging the people, composing the psalms, and making preparations for the building of the *Bet Hamikdash* in Jerusalem. None of these goals could have been accomplished by a man burdened by a depressing awareness of sin.

2. The phenomenon of impatience leading to doom is a recurrent theme in Jewish history: Adam and Eve tried to take a shortcut to attaining God-likeness by eating from the Tree of Knowledge. The people who demanded that Samuel appoint a king did not heed the prophet's warning that the moment was not ripe for a monarchy based on the Torah's royal charter. David "jumped the gun" by prematurely marrying Bathsheba and again displayed impatience in his ardent, premature desire to build the Temple in Jerusalem.

3. Two facts seem to indicate that there was unhappiness in Uriah's marriage to Bathsheba or that the marriage was never consummated: First, Bathsheba had no children by Uriah, whereas she conceived immediately by David. Second, Uriah stubbornly resisted the temptation of going to his wife during his two-day furlough. Furthermore, in certain situations, transgressing a Torah commandment may be permitted, if the violation is done *lishmah*, for the sake of God, for example, in the case of Esther. In the final analysis, we

rely on the talmudic statement that all professional soldiers in the army of David gave their wives a *get* (divorce) before going into battle. They did this to avoid the complications that would arise if they were to become missing in action.

4. This is not to say that the traditional approach of self-affliction should be completely avoided. In the early stages of *teshuvah*, when the *baal teshuvah* is torn by conflicting emotions and is still drawn to his former life-style, extreme self-affliction in the forms of shame, remorse, and fear of punishment may be the only way to overcome his passions. However, once he is securely settled in his new life as a *baal teshuvah* (and the damage caused by his earlier behavior is reversible), then the positive method of transformation, of turning former sins into sources of blessing and gratitude, is the preferred way.

David, the epitome of a *baal teshuvah*, never forgot that he sinned, and he reiterated this in many of his psalms. But he was not depressed or discouraged in his relentless efforts to set an example for *baalei teshuvah* of all time.

CHAPTER 5

1. Belief in the coming of *Mashiach* is one of the Thirteen Principles of the Jewish Faith, formulated by Maimonides.

2. Entitled "*Vom Sinne des Judentums*."

3. True to the Birnbaum style, Uriel saw the First World War not just as a political conflict but as a *Gotteskrieg*, "God's war," a war for justice and peace, in which the Austrian empire, where many nations lived peacefully side by side under the benevolent Emperor Francis Joseph, represented the ideals of tolerance and fairness.

CHAPTER 6

1. Salonica, 1522.

2. I heard this interpretation from the late Reb Issar Mazel, an Argentine businessman, founder of *yeshivot*, and an original thinker.

3. The Talmud then goes to the trouble of recording a number of parallels of the same idea, such as, "All trees will bear fruit each and every day." The skeptical student who claims that nature will never change is directed to a certain tree that produces fruit every day, even today.

4. The atom is conceived as a kind of dynamic particle, a store-house of indestructible energy waves that permeate space, progressing to the infinite realm of the *Kissei Hakavod*, the glory of the divine throne.

CHAPTER 7

1. Some thinkers believe that such *teshuvah* is insufficient since the experience of fear and awe of God is an essential ingredient of a full-fledged *teshuvah* and that without it, no true repentance can be attained.

CHAPTER 8

1. The present-day explosive advance in data-gathering capacity provides an illuminating insight into the progress of man's knowledge. Historically, scientific research was never impeded by a lack of intelligence on the part of contemporary scientists. In fact, during the past centuries science was advancing at a satisfactory pace. Problems did arise, however, in the second half of the twentieth century when scientists became inundated by torrents of newly discovered information. The growing volume of data overwhelmed the scientists, who found themselves confronting the impossible task of assimilating and interpreting mountains of data. More importantly, as scientific knowledge broadened, researchers discovered a connection between unrelated branches of science whereby medical science and biochemistry were found to be interwoven with astrophysics and quantum mechanics in an ever-widening grid of knowledge. As a result, researchers had to continually expand the area of their

investigation to include a host of data from extraneous fields that proved to be closely related to their own specialized projects.

Significantly, our generation is the first in history to have access to computers that have ever-growing capabilities and can digest and sort out the incessant flow of information, enabling us to solve some of the most baffling problems.

2. It is obvious that any attempt at creating a *teda* model for the *kissei*'s meaning in the remote realm beyond the finite universe is doomed to failure. According to the Bible commentator Malbim, our finite tools fail us when we apply them to the Infinite. In fact, the Torah explicitly cautions us never to forget that even at the revelation on Mount Sinai we did not see a divine image, not even with the aid of image-building tools (Deuteronomy 4:15).

If the prophet had employed current terminology, he might have expressed the concept of divine sovereignty in terms of a universal data bank into which are fed the myriad bits of information concerning the actions of all mankind. We could further expand the model of the *kissei* in the *teda* way by viewing the throne as a center of a huge mass of cables or conduits through which messages are relayed from mankind upward toward Heaven and from Heaven down to man.

3. In the Song at the Red Sea, Moses sings to God, "*Machon leshivtecha*" ("The place You made to dwell in, O God, the Sanctuary that Your hands established") (Exodus 15:17). Moses confirms that it is God Himself Who created on earth a site for a tangible presence, which suggests God being visibly seated on a throne. It may very well be that our sages alluded to this concept when they stated that *malchuta de'ara* (the government on earth) has its counterpart in *malchuta derekia* (the reign of Heaven) (*Berachot* 58a).

4. Since the soul has the potential to grow from lower to ever higher levels, it may be assumed that it has the capacity to reach out to the ultimate goal—the *Kissei Hakavod*. The *Kissei Hakavod* is the goal in the sense that the soul yearns for the nearness of God, as we say, "My soul pines for Your love" and "My soul thirsts for God, the living God; O when will I come to appear before God!" (Psalm 42:3). If this is so, then the two-way traffic that flows between the Creator and man would enable man not only to dispatch but also to receive messages from the realm of the *Kissei*—and this is important,

for it may afford him a measure of awareness of his personal record in the *Sefer Hazichronot* ("Book of Remembrances"), the celestial record.

This may be the thought underlying the wording in the blessing in the daily silent prayer, in which we ask God to grant us wisdom and discernment. We pray, *"Choneinu me'itecha dei'ah, binah, vehaskeil"* ("Graciously grant us the knowledge, discernment, and understanding *that comes from You*"). We are asking, in fact, for a minitransplant of divine knowledge to us. This divinely granted understanding allows us to obtain information about ourselves that reaches us and enables us to do *teshuvah sheleimah*, total repentance (the next *berachah*), as a result of our relationship with Him.

CHAPTER 10

1. We quote only those relevant to our discussion.

2. Every tenth animal among one's sheep, goats, or cattle born during that year must be set aside as a sacrifice to God. Animals born in one year cannot be counted together with those born in another for the purpose of tithing. The year for this purpose begins on the first of *Elul*. [Finkel]

3. The *Viduy* has been formulated in two accepted texts: the brief "*Ashamnu*," a list of twenty-four one-word sin categories, following the order of the *Aleph-Beit*, and the lengthy "*Al Cheit*," consisting of forty-two one-line formulations of sins, also following the order of the *Aleph-Beit*. (Both are recited eight times during the Yom Kippur services and once in the afternoon before Yom Kippur. The short version is also recited during the *Ne'ilah* (closing) service.)

The *Aleph-Beit* order of the *Viduy* symbolizes that our confession is supposed to be all-inclusive. The use of all twenty-two letters of the *Aleph-Beit* represents a comprehensive description of all possible human failings as they are expressed by means of all available basic instruments of our language.

Another essential point with regard to the confession is that when one has sinned against his fellow man, hurting him personally or financially (or when one has publicly sinned against the Torah), the persons offended or hurt (or the persons witnessing the public desecration of the Torah) must personally hear the sinner's confession. Since *Halachah* demands that a confession be communicated to the injured party, the repentant should have no doubt about his obligation to verbalize his confession to his Creator.

4. It is a pity that many worshipers at that late hour of the afternoon, toward the end of the lengthy *Mussaf* service, are exhausted by the fast and the lengthy prayers preceding the *Avodah* service, so that often they do not fully experience the high degree of devotion and inner excitement conveyed by both the text and the moving traditional melody of this climactic segment of the *Mussaf* service.

5. See Rabbi S. R. Hirsch's *Chorev* (Frankfort: J. Kauffmann Verlag, 1920) and his commentary on the Torah.

6. It is a talmudic concept that mankind is comprised of seventy nations.

7. Interestingly, the Pilgrims instituted Thanksgiving Day as an annual thanksgiving for the gift of their land and its bountiful harvest.

8. Outside the Land of Israel, the eighth day is the last day one sits in the *sukkah* (albeit without saying the blessing on this *mitzvah*), but the *mitzvah* of *lulav* and the *hoshanot* circuits stop on Hoshana Rabbah, the last day of Sukkot proper.

9. Rabbi S. R. Hirsch, *Chorev* (Frankfort: J. Kauffmann Verlag, 1920).

Even the *Mussaf* sacrifices of Shemini Atzeret did not consist of numerous bulls, as those of the first seven days of Sukkot did. Instead, only one bull was offered, as was done on Rosh Hashanah and Yom Kippur, certainly a hint that the closing days of Sukkot are intimately linked with the *tikkun* (restoration) concept of *teshuvah*.

Some chasidic leaders briefly tempered their rapturous elation by shedding copious tears at the height of the *hakafot* circuits. I remember when I was young, I was told by my late father how the Dzhikover *rebbe*, Rabbi Shiyah Horowitz, a descendant of Rabbi Naftali of Ropshitz (1760–1827), was carried away with joy as he danced the seven *hakafot*. Still, at certain passages his lustrous long white beard was drenched with tears. This happened especially during the fourth *hakafah*, when he fervently and passionately sang the words, "*Yodei'a machashavot hoshia na*" ("Knower of man's [banal] thoughts, help us now!"). These ardent, heartfelt tears so moved the hearts of his *chasidim* that they became a spiritual *mikvah* (ritual bath) that purified their thoughts and feelings, cleansing their souls. It was an experience they would not forget for the rest of their lives.

References

Alter, R. Yehudah Aryeh Leib. *Sefat Emet*. Pietrkow, 1905.

Arama, R. Yitzchak. *Akeidat Yitzchak*. Salonica, 1522.

Bereishit Rabbah, a midrashic work. Constantinople, 1512.

Birnbaum, Nathan. *Kadimah*. 1882.

Birnbaum, Nathan. *Selbstemanzipation*. 1885.

Birnbaum, Nathan. *Vom Freigeist zum Glaubigen*. 1920.

Birnbaum, Uriel. *In Gotteskrieg*. 1921.

Birnbaum, Uriel. *Das Buch Jonah*. 1921.

Cordovero, R. Moshe. *Tomer Devorah*. Venice, 1589.

Hirsch, R. Samson Raphael. *Chorev*. Frankfurt: J. Kauffmann Verlag, 1920.

Kagan, R. Yisrael Meir. *Mishnah Berurah*. 1892.

Kitov, R. Eliyahu. *Sefer Hatoda'ah*. Jerusalem, 1961.

Maimonides, R. Moshe ben Maimon. *Mishneh Torah*. Mantua, 1566.

Pesikta Rabbati, a midrashic work. Prague, 1653.

Rashi, R. Shlomoh Yitzchaki. Bible commentary. Rome, c. 1470.

Talmud. Tractates *Avodah Zarah, Avot, Berachot, Chagigah, Pesachim, Rosh Hashanah, Sukkah, Sotah, Yoma*.

Zohar. Tanna R. Shimon bar Yochai. Mantua, 1558.

INDEX

190

Index

ABOUT THE AUTHOR

Rabbi Chaim Nussbaum was born near Auschwitz, Poland, in 1909. Raised in Holland, he became a talmudist and mathematical physicist. He received ordination from the world-renowned Rabbinical Seminary of Telshe, Lithuania. His illustrious career as an educator, lecturer, rabbi, and scholar spans more than six decades. From 1940 to 1942 he was a rabbi and teacher in Java, Indonesia, where he also served as a chaplain for the Allied forces during World War II. He was subsequently interred in a Japanese prisoner-of-war camp. After returning from Southeast Asia, he published a cultural magazine, *Moriah*, in Holland, and taught at York University in Toronto, Canada, and schools in Cleveland, Chicago, and New York. He also traveled around the world studying the Jewish educational systems in such places as the United States, England, and Israel. He has written in English, Hebrew, Dutch, French, and German on topics ranging from Talmud, Bible, and philosophy to mathematics, education, and art. For twenty years he served as the principal of the Eitz Chaim Day Schools and High School in Toronto, and since 1979 he has been the director of the Moriah Foundation. Rabbi Nussbaum is the author of many books, most recently *Semblance and Reality: Messianism in Biblical Perspective* and *Chaplain on the River Kwai: Story of a Prisoner of War*, in which he details his experiences as a P.O.W. during World War II. Currently at work on several books about the Holocaust, the story of Job, the Talmud, and biblical personalities, Rabbi Nussbaum lives in Toronto with Rachel, his wife of fifty-six years. They have seven children, twenty-three grandchildren, and a growing number of great-grandchildren.